THE GOOD N
OF THE
GOOD NEWS

הבשורה של הבשורה

AN EXPLORATION INTO THE ESSENTIAL PERSONAL
IDENTITY OF BELIEVERS IN YESHUA

Ariel & D'vorah Berkowitz

Shoreshim Publishing

TIMELESS TORAH TRUTHS
דברי אמת התורה לעולם ועד

The Good News of the Good News

הבשורה של הבשורה

AN EXPLORATION INTO THE ESSENTIAL PERSONAL IDENTITY OF BELIEVERS IN YESHUA

By Ariel & D'vorah Berkowitz

ISBN: 9798386887520

Shoreshim Publishing
71040 Memphis Ridge Rd.
Richmond, Michigan 48062
Phone: 586-588-0193
Email: ad.tri@mac.com
www.torahtruths.com

Layout: Ruth Kulp   Email: dkulp4@gmail.com
Editing: Ariel's Nephew
Cover Design: Ariel & D'vorah Berkowitz
          Email: ad.tri@mac.com
Cover Layout: Jim Xavier
          Email: 1daytokyo@gmail.com
Cover Picture: D'vorah Berkowitz
          "Get yourself up on a high mountain,
          O Zion, bearer of good news." Isaiah 40:9

It is our pleasure to dedicate this work to our like-minded friends:

Tony and Ayalah Palanza
Who helped us to begin walking down this amazing new creation path.

Yoseph and Ya'el Kresefsky
Who courageously are bringing these truths to their congregation in Washington, New Jersey.

Ruth Kulp
An encourager who also brings these truths to her chavurah in Emmaus, PA.

Finally, in addition, we want to devote this work to precious friends in Taiwan and S. Korea, especially those who have allowed us to teach these truths many times through the past decades and who are endeavouring to apply these realities to their Home School Co-ops and other endeavors.

The following is certainly true for all of you:
"O how I love Your Torah!, it is my meditation all the day.

מָה־אָהַבְתִּי תוֹרָתֶךָ כָּל־הַיּוֹם הִיא שִׂיחָתִי:

Psalm 119:97

Acknowledgments

In 2022 we were asked by Torah Resources International – Holland to teach a Zoom seminar to help believers in Yeshua to know and understand their essential personal identity in Yeshua. It was entitled, "Are We Sinners Saved by Grace or Saints Saved by Grace?" This book is an expansion of the teaching notes we used for that seminar.

Other books we have recently published have followed the same process. *The Torah of the Sages* (2022) and *The Twelve Overlooked Prophets* (2020) were also expansions of our teaching notes for the same Zoom seminars in Holland. Previous to that, we held a seminar in 2017 that resulted in an audio/visual series called the *Mo'adim* (God's Holy Days of Leviticus 23). A complete list of all our books can be found at the back of this book.

Hence, we are extremely grateful to TRI – Holland for encouraging us to formalize our seminar notes into full books. Both of us are now formally retired, however, the adage is true that a teacher (and/or writer) never really retires! We are grateful to the Holy One of Israel for giving us the time, health, and support to continue writing and teaching into our golden years.

> "To Him who loves us and released us from our sins by His blood…" Revelation 1:5
> "Τῷ ἀγαπῶντι ἡμᾶς καὶ λύσαντι ἡμᾶς ἐκ τῶν ἁμαρτιῶν ἡμῶν ἐν τῷ αἵματι αὐτοῦ…"

Ariel & D'vorah Berkowitz
Arad, Israel
March, 2023

CONTENTS

Preface xi

Introduction xv

Chapter 1:
Inadequate Approaches to Defining Our Identity 1

Chapter 2:
Our Former Identity before Yeshua 7

Chapter 3:
From Darkness to Light, Part 1 19

Chapter 4:
From Darkness to Light, Part 2 33

Chapter 5:
God's Word and Neuroscience 51

Chapter 6:
Our New Identity 63

Chapter 7:
**Some Implications of Knowing
Our New Creation Identity** 75

Epilogue:
The Good News is Better than we Thought 91

Appendix 95

Bibliography/Helpful Sources 97

FREQUENT ABBREVIATIONS

ANE	The Ancient Near East
b.	The Babylonian Talmud
BCE	Before the Common Era (Corresponds to BC)
CE	Common Era (Corresponds to AD)
BDB	Brown, Francis; Driver, S. R.; and Briggs, Charles A. *The New Brown, Driver, Briggs, Hebrew and English Lexicon.*
BDAG	*A Greek - English Lexicon of the New Testament and other Early Christian Literature, Third Edition* (Bauer, Arndt and Gingrich)
EBC	*Expositor's Bible Commentary*
DSS	Dead Sea Scrolls
HALOT	Koehler, Ludwig and Baumgartner, Walter. *The Hebrew and Aramaic Lexicon of the Old Testament.*
ISBE	*International Standard Bible Encyclopaedia* (Revised)
LXX	Septuagint
NET	New English Translation
NICOT	*The New International Commentary on the Old Testament*
NIV	The New International Version
TOTC	*Tyndale Old Testament Commentary*
TNTC	*Tyndale New Testament Commentary*

PREFACE

"Get yourself up on a high mountain, O Zion,
bearer of good news.
Lift up your voice mightily, O Jerusalem,
bearer of good news.
Lift *it*, do not fear.
Say to the cities of Judah,
'Here is your God'!"

עַל הַר־גָּבֹהַ עֲלִי־לָךְ מְבַשֶּׂרֶת צִיּוֹן הָרִימִי בַכֹּחַ קוֹלֵךְ מְבַשֶּׂרֶת יְרוּשָׁלַ‍ִם הָרִימִי
אַל־תִּירָאִי אִמְרִי לְעָרֵי יְהוּדָה הִנֵּה אֱלֹהֵיכֶם׃

Isaiah 40:9

Isaiah lived about one hundred years before the tumultuous events that transpired with the Babylonian destruction of Jerusalem and the House of God, resulting in thousands of deaths and the captivity of those who remained alive. Isaiah not only spoke about those disasters but foresaw the return of many of those captives and their children from distant Babylon.

Though often overshadowed by the Exodus from Egypt, Israel's return from the Babylonian captivity is one of the most dramatic events in the Tanakh. When the venerable prophet spoke of that return, he described it in terms of a glorious deliverance, like a second Exodus.

Anticipating the return of the people of Israel to Zion, Isaiah also foretold that the special presence of God would come with them. Isaiah described the refugees' return to their beloved and sacred homeland accompanied by the special presence of God as nothing short of good news.

That is the thrust of the Isaiah 40:9 passage quoted above. In beautiful poetic imagery, Isaiah pictured the returnees repopulating the hills and cities of Judah. In doing so, it was as if they had climbed onto a high mountain in Judah to shout victoriously about their return, accompanied by the presence of their God (at least as many who desired to return). The word Isaiah used, which we translate as "good news" in 40:9, is the Hebrew term *meveseret* (מבשרת). Isaiah used the participle form, meaning "one who preaches good news." The Israelites, therefore, were the ones who preached the good news that they have come home to Zion with their God.

The Greek equivalent of *meveseret* (מבשרת) is the word *euaggelizo* (ευαγγελιζω). Both words mean "preaching the good news." This victorious-sounding word is used in the Scriptures to speak of what Yeshua accomplished in His death and resurrection on behalf of all who would trust in Him. The countless individuals who would trust in Yeshua can also be perceived as returnees. They have returned to the One who loves them and created them. What happens to those who trust Him is, for sure, nothing short of the best news anyone could ever imagine.

To be sure, life was difficult for Israel upon their return (it always is!), yet we can read their joy-filled testimony as follows:

> "When the Lord brought back the captive ones of Zion,
> we were like those who dream.
> Then our mouth was filled with laughter
> And our tongue with joyful shouting…"

Psalm 126:1–2

If it was that joyful to experience the good news of ancient Israel returning to their homeland, how much more joyful can it be for those of us who know the good news of the finished work of Yeshua? When we truly begin to comprehend the depths of what He accomplished by bringing us into the presence of the Holy One who brought us home, our joy is unlimited. As the Psalmist recorded, having been returned into the Father's presence is "like those who dream."

That joy is what this book is about. In this work, we will not only speak about Yeshua's work for His own people, but we will also explore some important details that are often overlooked about what He accomplished for His people. We will discover in greater depth the good news all of us have when the God brings us back to Himself. Those who are believers in the Lord know the message that they trust in as "the good news." This book is designed to help us understand what is truly good about the good news. We will see that the good news is even better than we thought!

.

INTRODUCTION

In the early 1980s, I (Ariel) was the main Bible teacher in a fellowship of believers in Yeshua in central New Hampshire. Though I had extensive training and experience as a Bible teacher, nevertheless, one day following a teaching session, a courageous woman, Linda (now Ayalah), asked to talk with me. She had heard my viewpoint several times about who believers are in Messiah — and it bothered her. I had been teaching that while Yeshua died for our sins, nevertheless, we were still sinners by nature. She had been taught that believers are new creations in Messiah in every sense of the term and she felt that my explanation of that concept was far from adequate, that I was missing the full thrust of being a new creation. Lovingly, yet confidently, she asked me to study the matter more assiduously. She (and her husband, Tony) waited patiently. D'vorah and I talked with this couple on multiple occasions over the next year, discussing key biblical passages related to the subject of our identity in Messiah.

We also had some help along the way in our study. Respected Bible commentaries crossed our paths, such as John Murry's *Commentary on Romans* and D. Martyn Lloyd-Jones's work entitled *Romans 6, The New Man.*[1] In addition to

---

[1] For complete information on all of these works, please see the bibliography/helpful sources at the end.

commentaries, we discovered several helpful books on the subject, such as David C. Needham's *Birthright* and *Lifetime Guarantee* by Bill Gillham. Then, we found some more popular works such as those by Neil Anderson, like *Stomping Out the Darkness.* Finally, let us not forget a helpful presentation for younger people by Peter Lord entitled, *Turkeys and Eagles.* There were more, but these studies proved to be the most influential. After scrutinizing the matter for over a year, D'vorah and I became convinced of the truth that our friends Ayalah and Tony were trying to share with us. It is a simple truth, not complicated at all: Believers in Yeshua are sinners no longer. Rather, we are saints saved by grace; we are new creations in Messiah.

Today, about forty years later, Ayalah and Tony remain some of our most steadfast and loyal friends and co-workers, helping to share the good news of the Good News to all who will take the time to listen. That good news is what this book is about.

You, The Readers

To be sure, we anticipate this book to have a very limited readership. We are not writing it for everyone. Our message is specifically for those who claim they trust in Yeshua of Nazareth and what He accomplished for them by dying for their sin and rising from the dead. However, in this book, we will not refer to such people as Christians, unless the context calls for it. The term "Christian" carries with it too much baggage in the 21st century, especially for Jewish people. Why do we need the term anyway? Rather, we will call those who say they believe in Yeshua as their Lord and Savior, "believers." They may be Jewish believers or Gentile believers. But we will simply call them believers.

D'vorah and I began writing this book in the early summer of 2022. From our perspective, humanity is in trouble — economics, politics, and health are just a few issues weighing on people all around the globe. Add the subject of identity to this list and we have a real mess! For the first time in history, some people do not know whether they are male or female. Gay rights and transgenderism are dominating many conversations and debates, flooding our schools, and finding their way into our legislatures. At the core of these discussions is the subject of personal identity. Moreover, some are also attempting to eliminate national and even ethnic identities. People truly are asking, "Who are we?" The subject of identity is affecting everyone from elementary school-age children to those of us who are in our twilight years.

This book will not address those important, controversial issues mentioned above. However, we most certainly desire to speak about another serious identity issue. We are convinced that if believers can confidently rest in their biblical identity, then they will be better equipped to wrestle with the other global issues mentioned above. That is why this is an important book to consider. We seek to answer the most fundamental questions any believer can ask: Who are we? What is our essential nature? What is our true biblical identity? Or, to quote the name of the seminar that inspired this book, "Are we sinners saved by grace or are we saints saved by grace?" How a believer answers these questions will help them determine how they think about themselves, the things they say, and the way they live their lives.

Not a Jewish Issue

D'vorah and I are Jewish people living in Israel. We value and treasure our Jewish identity. At the same time, we join countless other Jews who are asking, what does it mean to be Jewish? Is Jewishness an ethnicity? Is Jewishness based on religion? Perhaps both? Jewish people everywhere have been debating this issue for centuries, if not millennia. We will not solve that problem here. This book is not about Jewish identity. Moreover, we are not seeking to address other kinds of identity questions that Jewish people are asking.

Everyone wants to discover their own essential personal identity. The beginning point lies in the reality that we are created in God's image. That is the basis for discovering anyone's essential personal identity. It does not matter what religious label one gives themselves.

The New Birth — A Torah Issue

The issue of new birth is at the heart of knowing our identity as believers in Yeshua. In the 1st century, it was a Jewish concept with foundations in the Torah.[2] We see this in John chapter 3 where Yeshua was discussing the subject of new birth with Nicodemus. Yeshua rebuked Nicodemus, a known and respected Torah teacher, for not knowing about or understanding the concept of new birth.

This implies that the concept of the new birth was known in the 1st century from the Torah and/or the Tanakh. Yet, the Tanakh, for the most part, does not seem to use much of the same identity vocabulary as the Apostolic Scriptures when discussing the subject. However, just because the Tanakh employed a different vocabulary does not mean the concept of new birth was not a reality for the believers at the time. What Yeshua and Paul said about mankind's sin and inability was true for everyone. At the same time, God's provision for a new identity in the Torah has always been the same whether people knew the vocabulary or not. It has always been a work of God.

If one would like to explore the ways that our essential identity is spoken of in the books of Torah, we can suggest that the student goes to the Modular Biblical Training Academy (MBTA) found on this website: torahtruths.com (also described at the end of this book). The ways that God helps us to know what He created us to be is profoundly exciting to discover.

---

[2] The Hebrew word "*torah* (תורה)" means "teaching" or "instruction." It is unfortunately frequently translated as "law." It is one of the names the five books of Moshe use to refer to itself. For a more in-depth treatment of this word, see our book *Torah Rediscovered*.

A Vital Truth

In reality, it does not matter whether the concept of identity is a Jewish or Christian issue. The fact is, the knowledge about our true innermost essence is a *biblical* issue, and this should influence the decisions that believers make, how they act, what they think, and what they say. We hope that by the time you finish reading this brief study, you will also be in agreeance about how vital it is to know what the Bible says about our essential identity and are convinced about the difference it makes in our lives.

The Plan for This Book

We have divided this book into seven parts with each section building upon the previous sections. After the seven chapters, we provide a short summary, which we call an "Epilogue."

First, we will mention some inadequate approaches believers sometimes use hoping to establish their essential identity. Second, we will need to review our former identity as unbelievers. After that, in chapters 3–4, we shall examine what the Lord did for us to change us from that former identity. This issue will take up two chapters because there is so much information. In chapter 5 we explore how our present knowledge of neuroscience can help explain some of the dynamics of our identity in Messiah. In the sixth chapter, we will summarize what the Scriptures say about who believers are in Messiah, and because of Messiah. Lastly, we will explain some of the ways the subject of identity makes a difference in the lives of every believer in Yeshua.

A Few Preliminary Items

Before we begin with the main sections of this book, we have just a few practical notes to help guide the reader.

Yeshua and Moshe

We refer to Jesus by His Hebrew name, Yeshua, and Moses also by His Hebrew name, Moshe. The terms Jesus, Moses, and Christian will be used, however, if we are quoting someone.

Names for the Bible

Unless the context demands, or we are quoting someone, we will avoid using the traditional terms *Old Testament* and *New Testament* when referring to those sections of the Bible. The entire Bible, from Genesis to Revelation, is the only Divinely inspired Word of God, and referring to different sections as "Old" and "New" clouds the continuity of the material of those sections and confuses students about their nature. Instead, we will use the following designations when referring to different parts or texts of the Bible:

TANAKH

This is in reference to what is commonly known as the Old Testament. "Tanakh" תנך) is a traditional Jewish acronym: T–Torah, N–Nevi'im (The Prophets), and K–Ketuvim, the rest of the books, or "The Writings."

APOSTOLIC SCRIPTURES

This is in reference to what is commonly known as the New Testament because these books were all written by the Apostles. Once again, if there is a quote that uses a different name, we shall be faithful to the author of that quotation.

HEBREW OR GREEK SCRIPTURES

When referring to the original Hebrew Tanakh or Greek Apostolic Scriptures, rather than later translations, we will use the terms "Hebrew Scriptures" for the Tanakh and "Greek Scriptures" for the Apostolic Scriptures. (LXX, however, is the abbreviation used for the Septuagint — the Greek translation of the Hebrew Scriptures.

Furthermore, the following list ascribes which section of the Bible the specific books can be found. This division, particularly the ones in the Tanakh, follow the traditional Jewish way of delineating those books.

TORAH (תורה)

Genesis, Exodus, Leviticus, Numbers, Deuteronomy.

PROPHETS (NEVI'IM, נביאים)

Joshua, Judges, 1 & 2 Samuel, 1 & 2 Kings, Isaiah, Jeremiah, Ezekiel, The 12 smaller Prophetic Books.

WRITINGS (KETUVIM, כתובים)

Psalms, Proverbs, Job, The Five Megilot (Song of Songs, Ruth, Lamentations, Ecclesiastes, Esther), Ezra and Nehemiah, Daniel, 1 & 2 Chronicles.

THE GOSPELS

Matthew, Mark, Luke, John.

THE ACTS (OF THE APOSTLES)

THE EPISTLES (LETTERS)

Paul's Letters, Hebrews, Peter's Letters, John's Letters, Jude.

THE REVELATION

The categorization above recognizes that the Bible contains different kinds of writings, yet they all work together to form one unified book, God's inerrant Word, the Bible!

Quotations

We cite many different sources in this book, but that does not necessarily mean that we agree with everything that particular author thinks. Sometimes authors make brilliant statements that are too good to resist, and we enjoy referencing different authors for their helpful insights.

We think that is all the introductory material necessary to help the reader flow through this book. Thank you for considering our thoughts in this book. Happy reading and studying!

CHAPTER 1
INADEQUATE APPROACHES
TO FINDING OUR IDENTITY

Consciously or unconsciously, most people acknowledge that their identity is important. This assumption is borne out of simple observation. In Israel, where we live, we are confronted every day with people who consciously strive to portray themselves outwardly according to a certain identity — either religious, secular, urban, cosmopolitan, rural, simplistic, etc. Just consider the people in your own community and note how practically everyone makes some sort of effort to dress, act, speak, or engage with society in a manner that projects their chosen identity. (Even the simplistic "I don't care" effort is a conscious projection of identity).

If we stop and speak to people, most introductions and casual conversations would equally support the notion that people value their identity and assert it through various means. For example, if we randomly approach someone and ask them, "Who are you?" After they tell us their name, they might describe themselves through one or more of these means, most notably their profession, religion, or hobbies. Although these are great attributes to a person's daily activities, character, and accomplishments, they are not, we believe, adequate ways of discovering one's *essential identity*.

In this chapter, we will examine some of the inadequate measures by which most people attribute their identity. First, we will address arguably the most common measure, their profession. Then we will focus more intently on how believers in particular view their identity and approach identity questions.

Our Professional/Vocational Identities

Many people describe themselves through their profession or occupation. When asked, "Who are you?" They respond, "I'm a doctor," "I'm a secretary," or "I'm a homemaker." This is quite common, and many of us believers speak similar answers about ourselves. However, this approach to one's identity carries with it at least two problems.

First, the question is not "*What* are you?" but "*Who* are you?" If we state our identity by means of our occupation, it does not properly answer the question. Our answer might tell someone *what* the person does to earn money or *what* service someone might perform, but it does not state *who* the essence of the person is.

The second problem is, if we think of our identity in terms of our vocation, what happens if we get fired or lose the ability to perform that job? Does our sense of personal identity vanish with it? Regrettably, in some cases, many who cling to this identity do feel a sense of loss and they struggle to figure out who they are if they were to lose their job. With what, then, are we left to perceive of as our basic essence? Indeed, all of us have met people who find themselves lost when they cannot perform their profession any longer.

Our Ministry Identities

Believers in Yeshua often answer the identity question similarly. Too often they also think of themselves as identified by their occupation. However, they have incorporated a little twist to it. Some believers are involved in full-time ministry. They might be youth workers, pastors, councilors, or Bible teachers. Thus, if someone asks them who they are, they quickly respond by stating their ministry label or title. This essentially invites the same problems as above, only, the unfortunate little twist is, that somehow their occupation becomes rather religious or, for lack of a better term, spiritual. They are so involved in their ministry for the Lord that they consider this their identity — and it sounds good!

Both of these ways of perceiving oneself have a certain degree of validity, but, in the end, they fall far short of describing the true person on the inside.

Our Theological Identities

Some believers are more astute than others. They realize the pitfalls that come with identifying themselves with their work or ministry. They know better and are keenly aware of the problems associated with that kind of thinking. And yet, they have, nonetheless, acquired other faulty ways of thinking about their identities. The two most common are what we call "The Filter" and the "New Clothes" concepts, which we will discuss below. In doing so, we utilize examples from David C. Needham's excellent book on the subject called Birthright.

1. The Filter

The first example from Needham goes like this:

> God is absolute holiness and man is a sinner. Sin cannot associate with holiness. In order to help sinful man be in a right relationship with a holy God, God sent Yeshua. In Yeshua, God has inserted a miraculous filter between Himself and me, the sinner. That filter is Yeshua: His death, His resurrection. Therefore, as God looks down on me, He doesn't see me as I *really* am, but rather He sees all that is right about Yeshua (Italics ours).[3]

According to this view. God makes us judicially and positionally righteous because we have Yeshua covering our sin. When God sees us, he does not see the sinner. Instead, He sees Yeshua. But (and this is an important "but") at the core of this way of thinking, we are still basically sinners. Because this thinking assumes that God sees through a filter

---

[3] David C. Needham, *Birthright*, 46.

(Yeshua), we are positioned as righteous in His eyes, but in our own view, we are still essentially the same sinners we have always been on the inside

Thus, the problem with this explanation is that it declares our basic identity to be sinners, even though we are believers in Yeshua. What has changed?

2. The New Clothes

In our studies, we have encountered a second theological attempt to explain our identities in Yeshua that is similar to "The Filter" concept, but with a slightly different modification. This explanation reaffirms that we are sinners and God is holy. We cannot fellowship with a holy God. Therefore, God sent Yeshua. Through our faith in Yeshua's death and resurrection, God then "clothed" us in Messiah's righteousness.[4] Herein is the slightly different modification.

It is true that we are clothed with the righteousness of Yeshua. We read in Galatians 3:27, "For all of you who were baptized into Messiah have clothed yourselves with Messiah." Here we have it! We are, indeed, clothed with Yeshua. The problem is that this position is simply inadequate. It does not go far enough. According to this illustration, at the core, again, we are still sinners, yet in Messiah, God gives us a new set of clothes. He takes the dirty sinful ones away and gives us the righteous clothes of Messiah. But (another important "but"), at the core, we are still sinners, just masked with a new set of clothing.

3. The Position vs. The Experience

An essential part of those two pictures are two words that some theologians like to use when they describe who we are in Messiah. They like to make a distinction between what our *position* is in Messiah and what our actual *experience* is. In other words, there is a difference between our *standing* and

---

[4] We think this also is from Needham, but looking back through his books, we cannot find it!

our *state*. Our position, or standing, is that God considers us to be righteous because of Yeshua. Yet, our experience, or state, is that, though declared to be legally righteous before God, nevertheless, we are actually still sinners in our innermost being.

We may not think that all this theological thought has anything to do with us or that it does not affect us, but the truth is that it does. Even if the pastors and Bible teachers under which we have sat did not speak of these things directly, their teaching and preaching may have reflected these positions by the very wording that they chose. We may not be aware of how those teachings have affected us, but if we were to think about it, we would recognize just how much of our own identity concepts as believers has been shaped by these theological suppositions.

According to the above illustrations, our position and standing are that we are righteous, but our experience and state is that we are basically still sinners. This common, inadequate concept is worth repeating, as you will find that we do for most important concepts to help it really sink in. This idea is often expressed with pious sounding statements, such as: "I am just a sinner saved by grace," or, "I am just a beggar telling another beggar where to find the food." These sound good, *but are we really still sinners? Are we really beggars?* Doesn't Scripture tell us that we are royal priests? (Exodus 19:6 and 1 Peter 2:9).

Summing it Up

We are not denying the importance or enjoyment that comes from having meaningful conversations about our professions, or other personal attributes. Nor are we denying the allegorical lessons that be gleaned from either "The Filter" or the "New Clothes" illustrations. Rather, we are highlighting the fact that none of these common attributes or concepts really point to one's essential identity — especially for believers — and, if anything, they come with harmful faults. All we are saying is that there is more to what Messiah accomplished for us. In our new birth, our identity is completely changed, as well as our standing and our position before God. In other words, the good news of the Good News is better than we may have known! We will expand on this assertion as the book progresses.

CHAPTER 2
OUR FORMER IDENTITY

As noted in the introduction, the argument of this book is that believers in Yeshua are no longer sinners but saints saved by grace and new creations in Messiah. Our old identities may be couched in a sinful nature, because of the Fall, but our new identities are no longer tied to that nature. The essence of our identity, therefore, is not that we are still sinners, or viewed by God through a righteous filter, or wearing new righteous clothing to cover up sin. Rather, we are righteous in our essence because of Yeshua.

This chapter, however, is about revisiting our former identities. Not that we find it particularly healthy to bring up old wounds from our sinful nature, but because it is helpful to see more clearly from where God has brought us. In doing so, we will appreciate even greater what God has done for us in Yeshua. Beyond that, however, we will be in a better position to understand in greater depth the miracle God has performed for us by giving us a new identity. To help us through this part of the journey, we will examine two passages of Scripture: Romans 3:9–12 and Ephesians 2:1–10.

Romans 3:9–12

In the first three chapters of Romans, Paul established the reality that the entire world has sinned and falls short of the glory of God (Romans 3:23). He did this first by explaining that God has graciously provided mankind with enough revelation of Himself in His creation so that "man is without excuse" (Romans 1:20) for not seeking after who their Creator is. If people did, God would have revealed more of Himself to them. However, Paul explained further in chapter 1 that the nature of people is such that they rejected such revelation and "served the creature rather than the Creator" (Romans 1:25).

In Romans chapter 2, Paul focused on his own people, the Jewish people. He explained how they had unique advantages to know and to serve the Lord God (See Romans 9:1–5). Paul said these advantages are "great in every respect" (3:2). However, Tim Hegg, a gifted Bible teacher at TorahResource Institute,[5] reminds us that these advantages do "not mean that the Jew outshines the Gentile in every respect of life and being, but that the Jew has an advantage, a preeminence, which in every respect is great and important."[6]

Yet, in Romans chapter 2, Paul explained how "there is no partiality with God" (Romans 2:11). The Jewish people, heirs to the covenant relationship with God, are like others, they also have fallen prey to sin and became short of the glory of God. Indeed, the biblical narrative is full of historical examples of how the people of Israel have consistently violated the covenant relationship God established with them. Because of that, Paul admonished his fellow Jewish people by stating that "the name of God is blasphemed among the Gentiles because of you, just as it is written" (Romans 2:24).

Paul concluded in Romans 2:28–29: "For he is not a Jew who is one outwardly, nor is circumcision that which is outward in the flesh. But he is a Jew who is one inwardly; and circumcision is that which is of the heart, by the Spirit, not by the letter; and his praise is not from men, but from

---

[5] TorahResource Institute is an on-line Bible institute, emphasizing instruction the biblical languages, Hebraic backgrounds to the Scriptures, as well as other biblical subjects. This author was a part-time instructor for this school. By the way, the correct name is one word: "TorahResource!" See TorahResource.com

[6] Tim Hegg, *Paul's Epistle to the Romans*, Vol. 1, Chapters 1–8, 59.

God." In other words, true Jewishness is not merely a matter of ethnicity (physical descendants of Abraham, Isaac, and Jacob) but also a matter of fulfilling the calling the Lord gave to Abraham's descendants, to be a praise to Him as a nation.

Here Paul created a little play on words to sum up how the Jewish people have fallen short of God's glory. The word "Jew" in Hebrew is "*yehudah* (יהודה)." It is associated with a common Hebrew word for "praise." Paul, though writing in Greek, is nevertheless thinking in Hebrew, especially when commenting on his own people. He says, therefore, that though the people of Israel — the Jewish people — were called by God to praise the Holy One, they sought praise from people and did not live as a nation in such a way which would have brought praise to God, which was their national calling.

In chapter 3, Paul then focused on Gentiles, sometimes referring to them as "Greeks." According to Hegg, this might designate one of the "extremes of culture and education within the Gentile world."[7] Paul's assessment of the Gentiles is the same as that of the Jewish people. Accordingly, Paul said in Romans 3:9, "we have already charged that both Jews and Greeks are all under sin."

Indeed, the basic human condition of sin is not a Jewish condition, nor is it a Gentile condition. It is a pan-human condition. Paul summarized his position between 3:10–12 by describing mankind's problems — and he does so by quoting the Tanakh. This is to show that a sinful panhuman condition is not only assessed by the writers of the Apostolic Scriptures, but the entire Bible says the same thing about mankind's essential nature — it is totally enslaved to sin. How so?

No One is Born Righteous. Romans 3:10

"Righteousness" is a very important word in Romans. On the one hand it refers to judicial righteousness, where the Holy One judicially declares people to be acquitted for their

---

[7] Hegg, *Romans*, 18.

sins because of what Yeshua did for them. On the other hand, it refers to those whom God has declared righteous and will naturally walk a righteous life. They can do so because, as we shall see later, The Righteous One made them righteous inside.

As important as it is to be righteous, Paul stated no one is born that way and demonstrated that one cannot achieve the declaration of righteousness from God by being Jewish (through birth or conversion) or by being Gentile. Righteousness cannot be achieved at all! It is a gift that God bestows on those whom He chooses; merit does not enter into God's choice.

Outside of Messiah, whatever people think is righteousness, in reality, is not. It is only man's various versions of God's true righteousness. Apart from God, no man does good. Paul did not make this idea up. He is merely quoting from the Tanakh, from Psalm 14:1, to bolster his point. Hence, those who are not believers in Yeshua cannot call themselves "righteous." That is not their basic identity.

Most rabbinic thinkers today assert that people are born neutral. They make a conscious choice to become either sinful or righteous. However, rabbis did not always think this way. The Babylonian Talmud, Sanhedrin 101a, (written sometime between 300–500 CE) recalls a discussion about sin between the famous Rabbi Akiva and his contemporary, the equally famous Rabbi Eliezar ben Hyrcanus, both of the late 1st century and early 2nd century CE. Tim Hegg, commenting on this Talmudic interchange, remarks: "Thus, Hyrcanus, like Paul (and contrary to the majority of the Rabbis of that time) taught the basic sinfulness of mankind as over against the typical Rabbinic view that everyone is born 'neutral' and makes the choice to become sinful."[8] Furthermore, R. Akiva stated, "for there is not a just man upon earth who does good and does not sin." The conclusions that these two great Jewish sages came to basically reiterated what Paul was saying in

---

[8] Hegg, *Romans*, Vol. 1, 67.

Romans 3:10.

No One Truly Understands God. Romans 3:11

Paul continued to quote Psalm 14, this time verse 2, when he asserted that "There is none who understands; there is none who seeks after God" (Romans 3:11). He did so to support the assertion that sin has affected the way people think so much that even their understanding of God misses the mark.

The Greek word that the NASB translates "understands" is *sunion* (συνιων), associated with the verb, *suniemi* (συνιημι). This is the same Greek word used in the lxx of Psalm 14:2, which Paul quotes. According to one Greek-English Lexicon, it carries the idea of having "an intelligent grasp of something that challenges one's thinking or practice; to understand or to comprehend."[9] Hegg suggests that the word has to do with "religious or moral understanding."[10] Thus, Paul was not speaking about understanding things like science, literature, or history, but having an intelligent grasp on the moral nature of God.

Man may think he understands God, but, in truth, he knows very little, and even of that he really does not understand. People must rely on God to tell us about Himself. That is one reason why the Scriptures are so important. We hold to the truth that the Bible is the only Divinely inspired Word of God. If that is true — and it is — then the Bible is the only way to know the truth about God, because the Lord is telling us about Himself. Yet even when unregenerate men read the Scriptures they often do not understand or believe what God says about Himself, unless God opens their eyes to see and understand.

This thought is echoed in 1 Corinthians 2:14 where Paul says, "The man without the Spirit does not accept the things that come from the Spirit of God, for they are foolishness to

---

[9] BDAG, 972.

[10] Hegg, *Romans*, 67.

him, and he cannot understand them, because they are spiritually discerned." This does not mean that a person cannot have a rational understanding of truth apart from the illumination of his or her mind by the Holy Spirit. They can understand geography, mathematics, linguistics, etc. quite deeply. The passage is only referring to *biblical* truth.

Moreover, in one sense, a scholar can understand and explain theological principles just as well as any other area of expertise. An unbelieving philosopher can lecture accurately the biblical view of God. An unbelieving historian can analyze to near perfection the nature of biblical history and describe the meaning of justification by faith. Proof of this is that there are many excellent scholars on the faulty of Religion Departments in universities in the USA and Europe who are atheists! However, for many, these are merely just facts. If they have not put their trust in Messiah, they merely remain as facts and make little difference in their lives. In addition, they do not know what to do with the facts nor understand their depth of meaning and importance. It was as Dr. Bill Gillham notes, "The Bible will be meaningless to him in terms of being able to discern spiritual enlightenment from it. He may earn a Ph. D. in Biblical Studies but still not know anything about spiritual truth."[11]

Furthermore, even if there is a measure of understanding, people simply do not want it to impact their lives. Dr. James M. Boice, a godly Bible teacher who had a great influence on our lives many years ago before his death, shared an incident that illustrated this effectively:

> When I was at Harvard University there were non-Christian professors who could present the doctrines of Christianity so brilliantly that Christians would marvel at their lectures and be edified by them. and even unbelieving students would rise to their feet and applaud. But these

---

[11] Bill Gillham, *Lifetime Guarantee*, 68.

professors did not believe what they were teaching. If they had been asked their opinion of what they were so accurately presenting, they would have said that it was all utter nonsense... It is not that the doctrine of God...is difficult to comprehend. It is rather that we do not want to move in the direction these doctrines lead us. So, we suppress the truth about God, refusing to glorify or give thanks to Him, and as a result our thinking becomes "futile", and our foolish hearts are "darkened" (Romans 2:21).[12]

No One Really Seeks God. Romans 3:11

In the following passage in Romans 3, Paul tells us that no one on their own seeks after God. As much as some people say that they are seeking God, apart from God moving in their lives first, they do not seek after Him. The god whom unbelievers think they are seeking is, in reality, a god of their own imagination and not the one true God, the Creator of the heavens and the earth.

If no one seeks after God, then who can be saved or who can be in a personal relationship with Him? It seems that Paul is saying that sin has so affected mankind that even our wills are bound by it. Once again, let us turn our attention to Boice as he carefully and logically explains this to us. He asks, if our wills are bound by sin, then who is it who wills to come?

The answer is: No one, except those in whom the Holy Spirit has already performed the entirely irresistible work of the new birth so that, as a result of this miracle, the spiritually blind eyes of the natural man are opened to see God's truth, and the mind of the sinner, which in itself has no spiritual understanding, is renewed to embrace the Lord Yeshua the Messiah as Savior.[13]

To comprehend and appreciate this we need to remember

---

[12] James Montgomery Boice, *Romans (Boice Expositional Commentary)*, 294.
[13] Boice, *Romans*, 302.

that the One who sent His students into the world to tell others about Him is the same One that taught us, "No one can come to me unless the Father who sent me draws him" (John 6:44).

No One Does Good. Romans 3:12

Finally, this passage teaches that sin has so affected man that, "all have turned aside, together they have become useless; there is no one who does good, there is not even one."

Although writing in Greek, Paul would have had the Hebrew word *tov* (טוב) in mind when referring to the word, which is usually translated as "good" — the same Hebrew *tov* used during the creation story in Genesis chapter 1. If we look at how *tov* is used in Genesis 1, we will notice that at the end of each day of creation, God looked at what He had formed, and, pleased that it was exactly what He wanted, called it *tov*, or good. From this use of the word, we can understand that when things in the natural and human world function how God intended them to function, they are *tov*.

If we apply this meaning of *tov* to the Romans passage, we can see that looks become deceiving. Let us not mince the statement in 3:12 that "there is none who does good, there is not even one." In this case, many people might look like they are doing good, but whatever they are doing, according to Paul, is not *tov*, and therefore not what God intended.

If we do not relationally know God as the Creator, then we are unable know the good humanity that He intended. This is why the Bible often describes sin with the Hebrew word *chatah* (חטא), which means an act of "missing the mark" or "missing it." What is humanity missing? He is missing the knowledge of their Creator and the good humanity they were created to be.

Fallen man, unfortunately, is no longer that original humanity, which is why Paul stated that no one does good. Therefore, there must be new birth to bring forth a new creation in each of us that will brings us back to the *tov* humanity that God intended. Through the work of Yeshua, we have that new birth.

Paul continued in Romans 3:13–17, by saying that the effects of being inherently sinful in our essential core are total. It is not that a person continually sins all of the time. Rather, it is that nan's entire being is fatally affected by sin. Notice throughout this passage that all of man's being is affected: the throat, the tongue, the lips (3:13); the mouth (3:14); the feet (3:15); and the eyes (3:18). It is not that man in his natural state is as bad as he can possibly be, but rather that his entire being is adversely affected by sin. His whole nature is permeated with it. Human relations also suffer, because society can be no better than those who constitute it. Some of the obvious effects — conflict and bloodshed — are also specified (3:15–17).[14]

So far, things sound bleak. Perhaps we never thought of ourselves as being in such a hopeless and helpless condition, not to mention a serious identity crisis. Mark this, however: Things are going to get much worse before we speak of the good news! Accordingly, we move now to another important passage that speaks of the essential identity of those who do not trust in Yeshua — including us before we became believers in Him: Ephesians 2:1–10

Ephesians 2:1

We are still relying on Paul for one important element that describes our essential identity before God brought us to Himself. This element can be found in Ephesians 2:1, where Paul informs us that we were dead in our trespasses and sins.

The Greek syntax in Ephesians 2:1 is a little complicated. Paul is in one long sentence that does not find the main verb until 2:5 when we are told that God "made us alive." In 2:1 he uses a present adverbial participle to indicate our innermost condition which is the result of sin. Hence a better rendering

---

[14] These comments are based on a reading of Harrison's comments in: Everett F. Harrison, *Romans* (*Expositor's Bible Commentary*), comments on Romans 3:13–17.

of 2:1 might be "although you were dead by reason of your trespasses and sins."[15]

Furthermore, the participle is based on the verb "to be." Thus, the grammar of 2:1 is speaking of identity and points to our state of being before God made us alive in Messiah. According to Daniel Wallace, "The point of the text, in light of 2:1–10, is not to describe humanity in terms of attributes (such as wrathful children), but to speak of the hopeless situation of those who were without Messiah."[16] Ephesians 2:1 assumes our true moral, religious, and ethical condition to have been dead as a result of sin.

The Walking Dead

In medical school would-be doctors often study corpses. These are dead bodies lying on examination tables. They are poked and probed with needles and cut with knives. Not once would a student hear a corpse complain. They can attempt to tickle them or make an incision and the corpse will not respond. Why? Because they are dead! A corpse cannot respond to any stimulation.

It is the same way with the "walking dead." They cannot seek after God. They cannot understand God. Nor can they live a godly life the way God designed it according to His Word. That is how all mankind was/is without God. That is also why God must take the initiative to reach out to people first. John states it like this: "We love, because He first loved us" (1 John 4:19).

Summing it Up

Not living as we were created to be results in death. Thus, we read in Romans 6:23, "for the wages of sin is death…" This death is more than just physical (someday our bodies will die), it is a separation of our entire being from God for all of eternity. In short, we were born spiritually helpless. It

---

[15] *The NET Bible, Second Edition Notes*, comments on Ephesians 2:1.
[16] Daniel B. Wallace, *Greek Grammar Beyond the Basics: An Exegetical Syntax of the New Testament*, 101.

is helpful to let Dr. Boice sum up what we have been saying from Romans and Ephesians.

> The biblical view is that man is not well nor merely sick. Actually, he is already dead — so far as his relationship to God is concerned...If we are truly dead in our sin, as the Bible indicates...then we will find ourselves in despair. We will see our state as hopeless apart from the supernatural and totally unmerited workings of the grace of God.[17]

---

[17] James M. Boice, *God the Redeemer*, 29, 51.

CHAPTER 3
FROM DARKNESS TO LIGHT, PART 1

Chapter 2 was rather depressing. We did not like it either! It was difficult to recall the darkness that shrouded our identities before we accepted Messiah. It was even more difficult to realize that the dark inner condition of unregenerated mankind that Paul talked about in Romans and Ephesians is true for all outside of Yeshua. This chapter, however, will be different. Here we will explore some of the amazing things God did for us to change our identities completely — from darkness to light. But before we press onward with Paul's exploration of our new identity in Romans 6, lets first look at where the source of light in our identities really comes from. For this we have to turn back almost seven hundred years before Paul, to the prophet Isaiah.

Isaiah lived at a very dark time in the history of ancient Israel. He watched his fellow countrymen forsake the Holy One of Israel to follow Canaanite gods and goddesses and to participate in lewd Canaanite lifestyles. As a result, God sent the Assyrians and used them as a tool to discipline Israel. When the fierce Assyrian army made inroad after inroad into the Land of Israel, they brought further darkness, destruction, and death to the people. Since armies invading from Mesopotamia would enter Israel from the north, following the Fertile Crescent, the Galilee in northern Israel would have been the first place to feel and experience all these calamities.

Isaiah spoke about this heavy darkness when he described how the people felt as a result of the Assyrians' presence, and that of other foreign invaders:

> They will pass through the land hard-pressed and famished, and it will turn out that when they are hungry, they will be enraged and curse their king and their God as they face upward. Then they will look to the earth, and behold, distress and darkness, the gloom of anguish; and *they will be* driven away into darkness (Isaiah 8:21–22).

It sounds hopeless. However, Isaiah was brilliant with his words. He created this despairing verbal picture to help everyone appreciate the shining light that the Lord promised would come. Isaiah expressed it like this:

> But there will be no more gloom for her who was in anguish; in earlier times He treated the land of Zebulun and the land of Naphtali with contempt, but later on He shall make it glorious, by the way of the sea, on the other side of Jordan, Galilee of the Gentiles. The people who walk in darkness will see a great light; those who live in a dark land, the light will shine on them (Isaiah 9:1–2).

Later, Matthew 4:12–16 indicates that Yeshua is the great light Isaiah was talking about! Yeshua would begin His earthly ministry in the same geographical location that first suffered the darkness and gloom of Canaanite idolatry and the discipline of the Assyrian invasion. In fact, Isaiah predicted that the tribal areas of Zebulun and Naphtali would be the first to see that Light. Hence, it is no accident that Yeshua's hometown of Nazareth is in Zebulun, and Yeshua's Galilean ministry base, Capernaum, is in Naphtali. Yeshua, therefore, was the light to a land cloaked in darkness, and continues to be a light for those who live in spiritual darkness. Isaiah knew that his audience would appreciate the light of Messiah more if he contrasted it with the dark condition of the nation of Israel before Yeshua's ministry.

This historical condition of Israel contrasted with the ministry of the Savior; Yeshua, can serve as a grand illustration of what the Holy One would do for each life that would trust in the Messiah. We had to see that description of darkness painted by Paul in Romans chapters 1–3 to understand in greater depth why Yeshua had to come and what the Holy One did to change things.

That is the essence of this chapter in our book. We will now explore some of the amazing things God did for us to change our identities completely. To help accomplish this, we need to return to the Book of Romans and focus primarily on Romans chapter 6.

Just as Yeshua was a light to the darkness of the nation of Israel, as predicted by Isaiah and confirmed by Matthew, so He is the light dispersing the darkness of our former identities. But we wouldn't have known the all-encompassing intensity of that former darkness, and need for the light of Messiah, if Paul hadn't clarified it in Romans 1-3. Isaiah, Matthew, and Paul, therefore, complement each other in a grand illustration of what the Holy One will do for each life that trusts in Messiah. That is the essence of this chapter — to explore some of the amazing things God did to change our identities completely, from darkness to light. To help accomplish this, we now head back to Romans and focus primarily on chapter 6.

Union with Messiah — Romans 6

Justification by faith looms as one of the most important subjects in Romans 4–5. Chapter 5 opens: "Having been justified by faith, we have peace with God" (Romans 5:1). According to Dr. D. Martyn Lloyd-Jones, the theme of the rest of the chapter is "assurance and the certainty of salvation."[18] If we are justified by faith, we can rest assured that everything associated with faith, such as salvation, is going to be ours as well. Therefore, when Romans chapter 6 opens, it is easy to think that Paul has detoured away from justification to speak about other things, such as the doctrine of sanctification, as commentators often suggest. However, this is simply not the

---

[18] D. Martyn Lloyd-Jones, *Romans: Exposition of Chapter 6, the New Man*, 3.

case. Throughout chapter 6, Paul explains the great depths of what it means to have salvation and be united with Messiah. When Paul begins chapter 6 by asking, "What shall we say then...?" he was continuing the discussion of justification by faith from chapter 5 connecting it to the new themes of salvation and unity in Messiah.

Insightfully, Lloyd-Jones remarked about Romans 6:1 that if one teaches justification by faith alone, as Paul did, then he is more or less bound to be misunderstood.[19] This teaching opens the doors to vulnerable accusations of "easy believism" where some say that because we are justified by grace alone, it does not matter at all what we do; we can go on sinning as much as we like because it will contribute greatly all the more to the glory of grace.

Chapter 6 responds to such accusations by explaining in clear terms that such a notion is inconceivable for two reasons. 1) We are not the same person we were when we did not believe in Yeshua — we are utterly changed from the inside. 2) We are completely united with Yeshua in every way.

Paul provides further vital details about his assertion beginning in 6:2. It is critical for us to know the details because they help us understand how a person can be changed from being a sinner to a saint. The explanation has five parts. We will cover three of them in this chapter, then the last two in chapter 4. We break this up into two chapters so readers could follow it easier.

1. There was a Death Romans 6:2

As already indicated, Romans 6:1 begins with a pertinent question. Paul asks, "What shall we say then? Are we to continue in sin so that grace may increase?" The question is based on the faulty thinking that since we are justified by grace through faith, if we sin more, we will just get more

---

[19] See Lloyd-Jones' argument in *Romans*, pages 1–12. We have more or less summarized one of his key points in this paragraph.

grace. Apparently, some in Rome thought this. Paul calls out the foolishness of this notion in 6:2 when he says, "May it never be! How shall we who died to sin still live in it?" His answer begins as if he were trying to shout it from the mountaintops. In Greek, his answer is, according to Hegg, "a formula of strong denial and is found in Classical Greek as well.[20] Commentator Everett Harrison adds, "Other renderings are possible, such as 'Away with the notion!' or 'Perish the thought'!"[21]

Why is Paul so adamant in his answer? He tells us in the next phrase — and this is the key to it all. He says, "How shall we who died to sin still live in it?" In typical Jewish fashion, Paul answers a question with a question. In doing so, he throws the answer back to the ones who might be asking, as if he wants them to see for themselves the absurdity that believers in Yeshua should continue to live sinful lives after being justified by grace through faith.

Moreover, the above explanation that Paul supplied could come off as totally unexpected. He says a believer cannot live in such a way because he/she is dead to sin. That is the main point of the next few chapters — we are dead to sin. How can that be?

Romans 6:5 says, "For if we have become united with Him in the likeness of His death..." The Greek text does not have the words "with Him," as we read in the NASB. According to Hegg, the literal translation should be, "For we have become united in (or by) the likeness of His death..." Hegg comments on this by saying, "That is to say our union is such that we actually take on the likeness — we become one with the likeness of His death."[22]

The Old Man

Who was it that died? Paul says that the "old man" died.

---

[20] Hegg, *Romans*, Vol. 1, 132.
[21] Harrison, *Romans*, comments on Romans 6:2.
[22] Hegg, *Romans*, 141.

What is this that Paul calls "the old man" in Romans 6:6? To be sure, this term is difficult to define in fine details. Because of that, commentators offer several suggestions. For example, Boice says that the old man is "what we were in Adam before God saved us."[23]

However, in our opinion, Lloyd-Jones offers the clearest explanation when he asserts that the "old man" is,

> the man that I was in Adam [Romans 5], my old humanity… born in sin, born under condemnation, the man that sinned with Adam and therefore reaped all the consequences of the man who was under the wrath and condemnation of God…That man died with Messiah.[24]

We would simplify what Lloyd-Jones says like this. Simply stated, the old self (or old man) is not the old nature. The old self is the "old me," who has died. See 2 Corinthians 5:17, especially in the NIV: "Therefore, if anyone is in Messiah, he is a new creation; the old has gone, the new has come!"

We cannot overestimate the importance of the concept of being united with Yeshua's death. Paul states it again in 6:6 when he tells us that the "old man" or, as the NASB translates it, "old self" was crucified. In other words, Paul is beginning to explain what it means to be united to Yeshua.

Thus, the first aspect of our union with Yeshua is that we were united with Him in His death. In other words, in order for us to be changed from our old identity of being a sinner, God had to put us to death! God did not merely fix us, for we were not repairable; He had to put us to death. We know we are repeating ourselves. We do so because the truth of this seems so unbelievable!

2. There Was an Immersion. Romans 6:1–4

The next part of Paul's explanation of how we died to sin lies in 6:3–4. Here Paul reminds us "do you not know that all of us who have been baptized into Messiah Yeshua have been

---

[23] Boice, *Romans*, 667.
[24] Lloyd-Jones, *Romans*, 64.

baptized into His death?" (NASB). We need to understand what Paul means when he uses the word "baptize."

What Kind of an Immersion?

First, it is necessary to work with the translation. It seems that the translators throughout history merely took the Greek term *baptizo* (βαπτιζω), and transliterated it into English, making it read "baptize," rather than translating it. When the verse is translated, it reads like this: "Do you not know that all of us who have been immersed into Messiah Yeshua have been immersed into His death?

When people speak of immersion, they frequently refer to water immersion, such as when something or someone is immersed into water for ritual purification. However, ritual immersion of water is clearly not in view in our passage. Yet, the mere mention of the word "baptize" causes many people to revert to ritual purification in their thinking. Lloyd-Jones agrees when he remarks:

> It seems to me that many have missed this doctrine at this point because they have been diverted from it by the form of expression which the Apostle uses in presenting it. I mean, that having seen the word "baptized" in these verses, they never see anything else, and regard these verses as having nothing to teach except a particular doctrine of baptism.[25]

Water immersion as a ritual does not save people. It does not unite people with Yeshua. Rather, it can serve as an outward, visible *picture* of what God accomplished in the person, but is not a salvific act in itself. Lloyd-Jones contends, "that to argue that the Apostle has water baptism in mind in any shape or form here is to give a prominence to baptism that the Apostle never gives to it."[26]

One of the best biblical examples of what baptism might mean in this context is found in 1 Corinthians 10:1–2. Here

---

[25] Lloyd-Jones, *Romans*, 30.
[26] *Ibid.*

Paul writes, "For I do not want you to be unaware, brethren, that our fathers were all under the cloud and all passed through the sea; and all were baptized into Moses in the cloud and in the sea..." James Boice points out that the use of baptism in this passage:

> cannot be referring to a water baptism, because the only people who were immersed in water were the Egyptian soldiers, and they were drowned in it. The Israelites did not even get their feet wet. What do the verses mean? Obviously, they refer to a permanent *identification* of the people with Moses as a result of the Red Sea crossing. Before this they were still in Egypt and could have renounced Moses' leadership, retaining their allegiance to Pharaoh. But once they crossed the Red Sea they were joined to Moses for the duration of their desert wandering. They were not able to go back.[27] (Italics Ours)

Thus, we can say that to baptize means not only to immerse someone or something into water, but it also conveys the idea of becoming totally one with something or someone. In other words, in a context like Romans 6:3–4, to be baptized means be *identified* with something.

Immersed by the Spirit?

Lloyd-Jones suggests that in Romans 6:3–4 Paul is referring to Spirit immersion. He bases this on 1 Corinthians 12:13 which says, "For by one Spirit we were all baptized [immersed] into one body, whether Jews or Greeks, whether slaves or free, and we were all made to drink of one Spirit."

In 1 Corinthians 12:13, Paul is obviously speaking of an immersion other than water immersion. Again, the word baptize/immerse carries the idea of causing us to be identified with what happened to Yeshua. Hence, Lloyd-Jones says, "The Holy Spirit convicts us of sin, the Holy Spirit who gives us the principle of new life, who regenerates us, is the same Spirit who at the same time, joins us to Messiah; and this is true of

---

[27] Boice, *Romans,* 660.

every Believer."[28]

What are we saying here? When Romans 6:3–4 speaks about being immersed into Yeshua, it has to do with the Spirit of God causing us to be identified with Yeshua in His death, burial, and resurrection — to be one with Him in every part of His saving work.

Notice one more detail about this kind of identification. In Romans 6:3, the verb we are rendering as "immersed" in the Greek, is called an "aorist passive indicative." This means that, as an aorist, this verb speaks of something that happened once in the past, it is history; it did not keep happening over and over again. As a passive, it shows that we were acted upon by something or someone. We were the recipients of the action; we did not do it ourselves. This, therefore, would mitigate against baptism referring to any ritual.

Let us state this in slightly different terms. God's process of changing our identity is to unite us with the person and work of Yeshua. It was part of how He changed us from sinners to who He made us to be in Yeshua. Union with Messiah, is, therefore, the key element in forming our new identity. Note, for example, that the little phrase "in Messiah" or "in Him" is used frequently in the Apostolic Scriptures. One writer notes that this phrase is used 164 times in Paul's writings. Being "in Him" means to be united with Him. Another way of putting it is to say that we were/are united into Him.

Knowing that we are united with Yeshua, by means of the Spirit of God, is critical to understanding our new identity. This leads us to one final remark about 6:3–4.

Paul begins his argument in 6:3 by stating "Or do you not know?" We will say more about the dynamics of knowing, feeling, and experiencing later. But, from the beginning, it is critical that we *know* what God did for us. It is not critical that we wait for a feeling or an experience to happen.

---

[28] Lloyd-Jones, *Romans*, 39.

Let us move on in the passage to the next aspect of what God did to change our identity.

3. There was a Crucifixion.   Romans 6:6

How was the "old man" put to death? Paul answers that in Romans 6:6. He says that the "old man" was "crucified with Messiah." Lloyd-Jones, in conjuring up a common but disagreeable response to this notion, asserts that "crucifixion is a very long process, it takes a very long time, so what Paul is really saying is that the old man is undergoing this [long, drawn-out] process of crucifixion."[29] Many people think this way.

However, in Romans 6:6, Paul uses the Greek aorist tense for the verb translated "crucify." This detail from Greek grammar indicates that the crucifixion has already happened. It is not spread over a period of time. It happened once and for all to our Lord. Paul tells us that Yeshua's crucifixion was accomplished once in history. In like manner, therefore, it happened the same way for us because of our union with Him. Our old man, inheritor of Adam's sin, the man who was under the wrath and condemnation of God, was crucified on the tree with Yeshua. It is, indeed, finished!

Historians tell us that people simply did not survive crucifixions. "Because the Romans had a century or two to perfect this method of executing criminals by the time of Yeshua they were experts in ensuring the deaths of those they crucified."[30] Josephus cites an example of one who managed to survive. He, along with two others, was taken off the cross before he died. He survived, but the other two did not make it, despite the best Roman medical care.[31] However, according to authors Josh and Sean McDowell, the man's survival in

---

[29] This quote is from Lloyd-Jones, *Romans*, 63. However, just to be clear, Lloyd-Jones does not believe this. He is speaking this way as part of his rebuttal to this way of thinking.
[30] Josh McDowell & Sean McDowell, *Evidence That Demands a Verdict*, 246.
[31] Flavius Josephus, *The Life of Josephus*, 420–421.

Josephus's account "is seen as an exception."[32] "When it comes to Jesus of Nazareth and His experience on the cross, the result is most assuredly death."[33] Craig Keener explains further:

> Those bound with ropes often survived on the cross several days. The dying man could rest himself on a wooden seat (Latin *sedile*) in the middle of the cross. This support allowed him to breathe — and prolonged the agony of his death. When the soldiers needed to hasten death by asphyxiation, they would break the legs of the victims with iron clubs so they could no longer push themselves up; the skeleton of a crucified Jewish man recovered in 1968 confirms this practice attested in ancient literature.[34]

If the victim did not bleed to death, he suffocated.[35] When someone was nailed to a cross, it was such that he was forced to push himself up to get air into his lungs. If he could not do that any longer, because of weakness, he simply suffocated to death. If someone fainted, it was certain death. Liberal Bible scholars have been asserting for over a century that Yeshua merely fainted on the tree and was revived in the cooler tomb. That is an impossibility. When we are told that Yeshua died — He truly did die. It is a certain historical fact.

The death of the "old man" is also just as certain. Paul is saying that we were/are so identified with Him that when He died, we also died in Him. We were crucified with Him. It is actual. It is not theoretical. This is how the Holy One planned to change us. It was not to fix us nor remake us. Again, it was not just in theory. He actually put us to death. That is, He put the person who was a sinner to death when Yeshua died. Moreover, Lloyd-Jones reminds us:

> Let us never again try to get rid of the old man; he has gone. This is something we are to believe, and to receive

---

[32] McDowell, *op. cit.*, 246.
[33] *Ibid.*, 246–247.
[34] Craig S. Keener, *IVP Bible Background Commentary: New Testament*, 314.
[35] John Donahue, "Crucifixion," *Eerdmans Dictionary of the Bible*, 299.

by faith. This is not something you experience; this is something you believe; and it is only as you believe it that your experience will be triumphant.[36]

Moreover, Lloyd-Jones adds one more significant statement about the crucifixion of the old man:

> We are never called to crucify our old man. Why? Because it has already happened — the old man was crucified with Messiah on the Cross. Nowhere does the Scripture call upon you to crucify your old man; nowhere does the Scripture call upon you to get rid of your old man, for the obvious reason that he has already gone.[37]

As Paul discussed how we were transformed into a new identity, he used a few phrases which might be tricky to understand, yet crucial for unlocking how we were changed and how we can walk in our new identity. We are speaking of such expressions as "the body of sin," "the old man," and others. (We decided to treat these short phrases in a separate chapter. That will be in chapter 5.)

Our unity with Messiah is the foundation of our new identity. When the "old man" died on the cross with Yeshua, the darkness from sin in our identities vanquished, and our "immersion" into Yeshua replaced that darkness with light. Although Paul expressed these concepts nearly two thousand years ago, they are still the bedrock of our identify in Messiah. And, although he wrote nearly seven hundred years after the Assyrian conquest, as a Torah scholar, Paul's thoughts were certainly not far from the same concepts expressed by earlier prophets. In many ways, we as transformed believers are those same people whom Isaiah wrote about when he said: "The people who walk in darkness will see a great light; those who live in a dark land, the light will shine on them.

---

[36] Lloyd-Jones, *Romans*, 65.
[37] *Ibid.*

CHAPTER 4
FROM DARKNESS TO LIGHT, PART 2

This chapter picks up where Chapter 3 left off. It is a lot of material, so we broke it up for easier reading. In Chapter 3, we discussed how God changed us from sinners by birth to having the new life in Yeshua. So far, we have discussed and enumerated three factors leading to our new identity in Messiah:

- There Was an Immersion (Romans 6:1–4).
- There was a Crucifixion (Romans 6:4–6).
- There was a Death (Romans 6:2).

However, we need to bear in mind that our change was instantaneous. We are merely recounting the details of how God changed us as they are delineated mostly from Romans 5–6 and Ephesians 2. Let us now move on to factor number four.

4. There was a Burial.   Romans 6:4

Paul tells us in Romans 6:4, "Therefore we have been buried with Him through immersion into death…" (Our translation). Beginning this sentence with the word "therefore" indicates that it is dependent on preceding information — where Paul spoke about being immersed unto Messiah's death. In other words, Paul is about to provide one more detail about our union with Messiah.

What follows a death? Burial. As F. F. Bruce says, "Burial sets the seal on death."[38] Burial signifies finality. Paul says that we were identified with Yeshua's burial. When Yeshua was buried, we — the "old man" — was also buried with Him. The implication is that we have not only died to the former life of sin but have been buried to it. To go back to a life of sin once we have been joined to Messiah is like digging up a dead body. Why would a person ever want to do that? Hence, Paul wants to impress on us the fact that we cannot ever think of ourselves as people with a sinful nature. The "old man" and "sinful nature" are both dead and buried! (Note, by the way, how we equate the phrase "old man" with the expression "sinful nature").

A Different Kingdom

Being buried with Messiah also signifies something else. It reminds us that before we were dead and buried with Yeshua (when we were sinners) we belonged to a different kingdom. As Paul stated:

> For if by the transgression of the one, death reigned through the one, much more those who receive the abundance of grace and of the gift of righteousness will reign in life through the One, Yeshua the Messiah…so that, as sin reigned in death, even so grace would reign through righteousness to eternal life through Messiah Yeshua, our Lord (Romans 5:17 and 21).

The use of the term "reign" hints that Paul is speaking of kingdoms — in this case, two kingdoms. In one kingdom, we were completely under the domain of sin and death. They ruled us. We had to do their bidding. However, Paul goes on to announce that when we trust in Yeshua and are united with Him in His death and burial, we leave the kingdom of sin and death and enter a completely different kingdom — that of grace and righteousness. (More on this kingdom soon.) Lloyd-Jones conveys this concept perfectly when he says:

---

[38] F. F. Bruce, *Romans* (*Tyndale Commentaries*), 141.

So, it is true to say of us that, as a man when he dies and is buried has entirely finished with this realm and life in which we live, so when we were buried with Messiah it was the final proof of the fact that we also have finished with the reign and the realm and the rule and the power of sin.[39]

Let us progress in Romans 6 and examine what else God did to make us new creations.

5. There Was a Resurrection. Romans 6:5–11

Romans 6:5 emphatically states, "For if we have become united with Him in the likeness of His death, certainly we shall also be in the likeness of His resurrection." Our likeness in His resurrection is one of the most glorious truths in all of the Bible. Paul spends more time in these verses speaking about Yeshua's resurrection than anything else in order to emphasize that we have a new life through our union with Yeshua. Let's break this concept down and explore it in greater detail.

A New Union

We touched briefly on our union with Messiah in Chapter 3, but here we re-visit the idea from a different angle.

The Greek word that the NASB translates "united with" is *sumphutoi*, (συμφυτοι).[40] In secular Greek literature it was often an agricultural word, speaking of plants that are grown together.[41] From this use, the term morphed into conveying the idea of "being associated in a related experience ('grown together')."[42] Commentator Alan Johnson writes that in Romans 6:5, "Paul uses an expression here, translated 'united with,' that strictly means 'grown together,' virtually with the

---

[39] Lloyd-Jones, *Romans*, 47.

[40] Greek students can easily see this is a compound word. The first part is the preposition *sum*, συμ. This is where we get the idea of "with."

[41] James Hope Moulton and George Milligan, *The Vocabulary of the Greek Testament*, 599.

[42] BDAG, 960.

force of 'fused into one.'"[43]

Essentially, Paul used two words to speak of our union with Messiah. First, from 6:3–4, we were immersed into Yeshua. Being immersed is one way of depicting our union with Him because when something is immersed into water it essentially becomes one with the water. Then, from 6:5, Paul said the same thing but with the phrase: "united with." The text also uses the verb "to be" in the Greek perfect tense. According to Johnson, this verb tense clearly denotes that "this union is not something gradually arrived at through a process of sanctification."[44] Rather, the perfect tense indicates that our union with Messiah is a fact accomplished in the past with continual results in the present. Yet, the verse also looks to the future by using a future tense verb, assuring us that while we are united with the living Messiah right now, sharing Yeshua's life inside of us, in the future our bodies will also be resurrected like His. Thus, our whole entire being will be just like Him in His physical resurrection.

A New Existence

Sharing Yeshua's life inside of us and being united with His resurrection also implies that we have left our old life. Paul states in 2 Corinthians 5:17: "Therefore if anyone is in Messiah, he is a new creature; the old has passed away; behold, the new have come" (Translation ours).

The old that has passed away is our old sinful nature — the "old man." Paul is merely repeating the concepts in 2 Corinthians 5:17 which he spoke of in Romans 6. The verb translated "passed away" means "to be no longer available" or "to come to an end and so no longer be there."[45] Moreover, the verb is in the aorist tense, which as we have indicated earlier, tells us that whatever passed away, and is no longer there, is history! It is completed action in the past. When we

---

[43] Alan F. Johnson, *Romans* in *The Expositor's Bible Commentary* (EBC), comments on Romans 6:5.
[44] *Ibid.*
[45] BDAG, 776.

are told that the new has come, the verb has to do with something being created.[46] The tense of this verb is perfect, which means that it is a completed action with continuing results in the present. The language therefore suggests that a new life has been created — and it continually exists.

Elsewhere, this concept is spoken of in terms of a new birth — born again or born from above. The Apostolic Scriptures use both expressions. John uses the Greek word, *anothen* (ανοθεν) in John 3:3, which can mean either "again" or "from above."[47] Peter uses the word *anagennesas* (αναγεννησας) in 1 Peter 1:23, which literally means "born again." Both concepts are valid. In truth, one who is born again is born from above. The new life he/she has is completely from God. In 2 Corinthians 5:17, we saw that "if anyone is in Messiah, *he is* a new creature; the old things passed away; behold, new things have come." A person is born that never existed before — a new creation was created!

A New Kingdom

Since we now have a new existence because Yeshua lives in us, and we are united with Him, we are now part of another, different kingdom. As already mentioned, the language in Romans 5:12–21 suggests we were serving a kingdom of sin and death before we trusted in Yeshua. Evil rulers of that kingdom dictated what we had to think, say, and do. We had no choice; we had to do their bidding. We were their slaves. We were slaves to sin and death.

Things are completely different now. We are in a new kingdom. Colossians 1:13 says, "For He rescued us from the domain [kingdom] of darkness and transferred us to the kingdom of His beloved Son." It could not be more clear! We now have a new king — Yeshua, the One who loves us.

Now, in Messiah, whenever our old master, sin, makes its plea, we can say, "No!" Romans 6:6 tells us that God united us

---

[46] BDAG, 197.
[47] BDAG., 92.

with Yeshua's resurrection, "so that we would no longer be slaves to sin." To be sure, sin frequently makes its demands known. We call these temptations. Moreover, when we hear these pleas in our minds, they sometimes even sound like our voice! This is where knowing biblical truth is essential. This is where we need to remember that our old man is dead and gone. However, sin sometimes attempts to lure us by speaking to our minds with a voice that sounds like ours. According to the Word of God, we are under no obligation to listen to that old master. We can say, "No!"

A New Kind of Death

Romans 6:9 says that "death no longer is master over Yeshua." He defeated death as we know it. It is true that our physical bodies will eventually die, but the life of Yeshua in us never dies. However, the text says more. It says that Yeshua was raised from the dead. He defeated even physical death. That is what a resurrection is. A resurrection means that although our physical bodies pass away, someday they too will be raised up again. That is exactly what happened to Yeshua, and is what, one day, will happen to us.

Moreover, when our bodies are raised up, they will be different. They will not be affected by sin, decay, imperfections, sicknesses, etc. — just like Yeshua's resurrected body. And yet, resurrected bodies are still completely physical. We can say that in the resurrection, God will restore our bodies to be what they were when He first created mankind. Hence, when believers in Yeshua die, our death is unlike that of all others. We experience the loss of our bodies, yet when we breathe our last, we have the assurance that someday our unseen selves, will be united with a resurrection body before we know it!

It is very similar to waking up from surgery. Before the medical procedure, we were anxious, perhaps even fearful of what the operation would be like. Then the anesthesiologist puts us out. We might be out for hours. But then we wake up, not knowing anything of what happened in the surgery. When we wake, it is as if we were never out. We imagine that this experience might be quite similar to death. We might face it with a little trepidation, not knowing what we might experience. But then we are awake again, and with a new life. It is as if nothing happened.

The difference is a totally new existence. Paul teaches us that we are seated with Messiah in the heavenlies (Ephesians 2:6). All we wait for is a new body that will come at the resurrection. Being united with Yeshua in His death is a guarantee that we will also rise with Him (Romans 6:5).

We would like to share a precious story that we heard many years ago from the late Dr. Donald Grey Barnhouse, a renowned Bible teacher of a previous generation.[48] it is about his wife's death and how he helped his children understand the difference in death for one who is in Messiah and one who is not.

He and his children were on a road trip driving through a mountain pass. An oncoming truck was about to pass them on the left. But, because of the angle of the sun, the shadow of the truck projected along the mountain side to their right. Dr. Barnhouse told his children to watch as the actual truck passed them on their left, but the shadow of the truck passed over them and projected up the mountain side on their right

At that moment Dr. Barnhouse said, "Children, you saw the truck passing us and we were hit with the shadow of the truck." So, he asked them, "would you rather be hit by the truck or by the shadow of the truck?" They all quickly said, "Oh daddy, by the shadow of the truck!" Then he said to his children, "That is what happened to mommy. Yeshua was hit by the truck and mommy was hit by the shadow of the truck." He went on to explain about what Yeshua did for us. He had spoken this so many times before, but this time was special because of the visual of the truck and the reference to the

---

[48] In truth, we did not hear this story directly from Dr. Barnhouse's mouth. Rather, in the early 1970s we heard Dr. James M. Boice relate the story in a sermon he was preaching.

children's mother. He helped his children to understand that this is something of what Psalm 23:4 means when it says: "Though I walk through the valley of the shadow of death, You are with me."

Think about how profound it is that Yeshua's finished work on the Tree returned us to life in Him — and we will never again be outside of that reality. For the remainder of our life, we are inside Him here on earth and inside Him seated now in the heavenlies. This is a dual reality. When the time comes for us to leave this world, we already are IN HIM at the very moment when we breathe that last breath, and we pass through to our unseen reality. That has been our reality since our new birth, born from Above! When we who are IN HIM, breathe our last breath, we pass from LIFE IN HIM to LIFE IN HIM. This also is one of the results of the finished work of Messiah on the Tree. Oh, the wonder of it all!

A New Certainty

Paul makes another remarkable statement about being united with Yeshua's resurrection. He says in Romans 6:9 that when Yeshua was raised from the dead, He "is never to die again." Paul is saying that death no longer has any power over Yeshua. He would never again experience death. Sin is ultimately what caused all human death. When Yeshua defeated sin by dying for it and taking it away from us, Paul informed us that "the death that He died, He died to sin once for all" (Romans 6:10). The emphasis is on "once for all." Then, in Romans 6:11, Paul makes the glorious application to all who trust Him. He says, "Even so consider yourselves to be dead to sin, but alive to God in Messiah Yeshua."

Therefore, when Yeshua was raised from the dead, He "is never to die again." And because we are in Him, we will never experience death like those who are not in Him.

All of this gives rise to an important question often posed by those who do not understand Romans 6: "Can a believer lose his/her salvation?" That is a reasonable, yet misguided, question. The question should be: "Can we die again?" After all, when someone suggests that salvation can be lost, what they are really saying is that life can be lost, and death can rule again.

Yeshua's resurrection proves that dying again is an impossibility. Salvation is not something that we acquire along the way, like a new piece of clothing. It is something we have as a gift from God's mercy and grace. But more than that, it is something we have *become*. We have become people who are alive forever because we are united with the living Yeshua. Since Yeshua cannot die again, we, therefore, cannot die again. We are forever united with Him in His death, burial, and resurrection. It is an inseparable union.

Moreover, the person who was deserving of death — our former sinful identities, or the "old man" — has died once and for all. Not only did we die to sin, but the sinner died also. The certainty of our eternal life is sealed with the reality that we are united with Yeshua. We are in Him, and He is in us.

This leads us to explore the final implication of the resurrection.

A New Place

Psychologist Bill Gillham insightfully writes, "Salvation is a two-sided coin. Side A represents Jesus coming into the believer; side B represents believers coming into Jesus. He is in me, and I am in Him. This is a package deal; you can't get one side at a time."[49]

We have previously stated that Paul used the phrase "in Him," "in Yeshua," or "in Messiah" about 164 times in his letters. Here is just a sampling of the kind of identity statements that are true for us because of this union with Yeshua:

- We are *Chosen* in Him (Ephesians. 1:4).
- In Him we are *Redeemed* (Ephesians. 1:7).
- In Messiah we are *Justified* (Galatians 2:17).

---

[49] Gillham, *Lifetime Guarantee*, 71.

- We are *Sanctified in Messiah* (1 Corinthians 1:2).
- We are *Enriched* "in Him (1 Corinthians 1:5).

Moreover, let us not forget Yeshua's profound prayer before He was crucified in John 17:21. He prayed to His Father, on behalf of those who would trust Him "that they may all be one; even as You, Father, are in Me and I in You, that they also may be in Us, so that the world may believe that You sent Me." We are in Him, and He is in us. That means we are in a new place. At the end of Yeshua's statement, he says, that by living out our union with Him while we are in this world, we will bring glory to God and people will come to believe in Yeshua.

As we have already stated, being in Yeshua is not like a piece of clothing to put on or take off. It is a place. The type of place He provides for us can be pictured by the 1960s Broadway musical (turned into a movie) *West Side Story*. In this musical, a love story takes place on the west side of the crowded inner city of New York City. However, the lovers are star-crossed. They are from different cultural backgrounds and forces in their societies worked against their relationship. It is like a modern version of *Romeo and Juliet*.

One of the most touching scenes is where the lovers sing together the song, "There is a Place for Us." Their worlds attempted to crush their relationship. Yet they both drew solace in knowing that "someday there is a place for us." Here are the words. This beautiful song features the star-crossed lovers Tony and Maria singing alternately to each other:

> There's a place for us,
> Somewhere a place for us.
> Peace and quiet and open air
> Wait for us, somewhere.
>
> There's a time for us,
> Someday a time for us,
> Time together with time to spare,
> Time to learn, time to care

Someday!
Somewhere!
We'll find a new way of living;
We'll find a way of forgiving.
Somewhere!

There's a place for us,
A time and place for us.
Hold my hand and we're halfway there.
Hold my hand and I'll take you there

Somehow,
Some day,
Somewhere![50]

What a song of hope! Yet, it is even better with Yeshua! *West Side Story* was a fictional story (although we are sure that there are relationships which also have had such difficulties). However, many people think and feel that there is no place for them in the universe. The Good News is that there is a place. That place is in Messiah. It is a safe place. It is a holy place. It is a place where there is a personal relationship, where love never ever ends! Moreover, we believe that everyone deep down knows that such a place exists, yet they do not know how to get there.

The Scriptures speak of a special place of God's presence. For example, when Israel came out of Egypt, they sang a song to their Redeemer recorded in Exodus 15:17. "You will bring them and plant them in the mountain of Your inheritance, the *place*, O Lord, which You have made for Your dwelling..." (italics ours). Then, as they were about to enter the Land of Promise following their forty-year wandering, Moshe said to the Israelites, "But you shall seek the Lord at *the place* which the Lord your God will choose from all your tribes, to establish His name there for His dwelling, and there you shall come"

---

[50] Music by Leonard Bernstein, lyrics by Stephen Sondheim. © 1956, 1957 Amberson Holdings LLC and Stephen Sondheim. Copyright renewed. Leonard Bernstein Music Publishing Company LLC, Publisher.

(Deuteronomy 12:5, italics ours).

At this same occasion, Moshe declared to the people "The eternal God is a dwelling *place*, and underneath are the everlasting arms..." (Deuteronomy 33:27, italics ours). Here we see that God Himself is a special place. He is a secure place for His people. Indeed, elsewhere, the Psalm writer declares to the Lord, "You are my hiding *place*; You preserve me from trouble. You surround me with songs of deliverance. Selah." (Psalm 32:7, italics ours).

The Hebrew word that we translate "place" is *makom*, (מקום). Sometimes modern Jewish thinkers speak of God as "*haMakom*, (המקום)" ("The Place"). They say it is one of God's names. For example:

> When used in reference to [God] what it means is that everything is contained within [God] (conceptually), while He is not contained in anything. As our Sages say: "He [God] doesn't have a place, rather He is The Place of the Universe."[51]

For those of us who are born from above, we are in Him, so He is our place of dwelling.

Reasons why people often seek a unique place for themselves to fit-in to this world include the need to feel special, protected, and secure. This makes sense considering that God created each person in humanity to be special, protected, and secure. So, naturally, we all have the inherent need to seek those securities. As the Creator, God, intended for Himself to be that Place for those that He created. For sure, as mentioned above, the Scriptures hint that God is that special place when Yeshua prayed for His people in John 17:21-23. We are in God, and He is in Us. This is not something that we merely have, it is part of our deepest identity — we are those who are intimately united with Our Father through the Son and are placed in the most sacred place of all — in Him.

---

[51] https://ohr.edu/ask_db/ask_main.php/37/Q1/

Not Something, But Someone

There is another implication of being united with Yeshua in His resurrection. Ephesians 1:3 says that because we are in Him, we have been blessed with "every spiritual blessing in the heavenly places." Then, in Ephesians chapters 1–3, Paul outlines some of those blessings that were given to us by God's grace when we believed in Him.

However, Paul is not saying that we *have* something new. He teaches us that we *have become* united with Yeshua's resurrection, and therefore we *have become* someone new. David Needham states it clearly when he says, "What you *have* isn't the point. It's *who you are* that's the issue."[52] Indeed, by being united with Messiah's resurrection we have become something we have never been before — we have become alive for the first time!

Extra Features

Before concluding our exploration of Romans 6, we would like to comment on two special features that will make a big difference in how we understand these passages in Scripture.

1. The Verbs

Throughout Romans 6:1–11, Paul's makes an important use of two particular Greek verb tenses: the perfect tense and the aorist tense. We have already touched on this briefly. Biblical Greek has at least four major ways of expressing something that happened in the past: the pluperfect, perfect, aorist, and imperfect. We will only focus on the perfect and aorist tenses because they play a significant role in Romans 6.

As far as the aorist tense is concerned, biblical Greek grammar expert Daniel B. Wallace stated that Paul used this tense frequently in Romans 6:1–11 since it is describing events that historically happened in the past, once for all. In regard to the perfect tense, Wallace says:

---

[52] David C. Needham, *Birthright*, 64.

the primary uses of the perfect are fairly easy to comprehend, though they are not insignificant...the perfect tense is "the most important, exegetically, of all the Greek Tenses... The force of the perfect tense is simply that it describes an event that, completed in the past (we are speaking of the perfect indicative here), has results existing in the present time (i.e., in relation to the time of the speaker).[53]

We place such emphasis on technical Greek grammar because Paul used both the perfect and aorist tenses in Romans chapter 6 to emphasize the historicity of Yeshua's death, burial, and resurrection, and the certainty of our union with Him in each of these. Let us have a closer look at the uses of these tenses in Romans chapter 6.

- We died to sin (aorist), 6:2.

- We were baptized into Messiah (aorist), 6:3 (2x).

- We were buried with Messiah (aorist), 6:4.

- Messiah was raised from the dead (aorist), 6:4.

- The Old Man was crucified with Messiah (aorist), 6:6.

- We were freed from sin (perfect tense), 6:7. (Note the perfect tense here, showing that not only was Yeshua's event historical, but there are continuous results of that affect us right now in the present.)

- We died with Messiah (aorist), 6:8.

- Messiah died (aorist), 6:10.

This list shows a very consistent use of the aorist tense. It shows that Paul is speaking about history. He is not just denoting possible or theoretical events. He is speaking of definite historical events concerning the work of Yeshua, and,

---

[53] Wallace, *Greek Grammar Beyond the Basics*, 573.

therefore, the validity of our connection with Him. He is also speaking of something Yeshua accomplished for His own, not merely making something possible.

2. The Role of Truth

Earlier, we mentioned the role of knowing the truth and not waiting for some personal experience to verify it. We would like to expand on that here by looking at how many times the words "know," "consider," and "trust/believe" are used in the short passage of Romans 6:1–11.

- **Don't you know** we were immersed into Messiah? (6:3).
- **Knowing this**, that the Old Man was crucified with Messiah (6:6).
- **We trust/believe** that we shall be raised with Messiah (6:8).
- We are **to consider** ourselves to be dead to sin (6:11).

We can see that Paul exhorts us to think correctly about ourselves. He does not tell us to wait until we feel our union with Yeshua, nor bid us to *experience* it before we know it is true. Rather, Paul — as always — instructs us to let the truth permeate our minds. He wants us to be guided by the mind of Messiah which says that we are to know ourselves as united with Him. It is on the basis of that knowledge that we are to trust it to be true.

Moreover, Bruce astutely comments, "This is no game of 'let's pretend'; believers should consider themselves to be what God in fact has made them."[54] Our union with Messiah is not theoretical, nor a mere possibility. It is very real. It is who we are. There is no need to pretend it into being.

Lloyd-Jones also helps explain the significance of these statements:

---

[54] Bruce, *Romans*, 143.

Whatever your experience, whatever your feeling may be, I tell you this; if you are a believer, you are complete in Messiah. He is now your wisdom, your righteousness, your sanctification, and your redemption. Now!

You may go on to experience these things more and more, and we should do so. That is why we need to be taught, that is why we need to be exhorted to apply what we have learned; but that does not make any difference to the fact. What the Apostle is saying here is this: You are no longer in Adam, you are in Messiah; and if you are in Him, what is true of Him is true of you.[55]

What is true of Him as the second Adam, is true of us (See Romans 8:29). We can experience this truth if we grow a mind that matches our new reality. The Creator designed our feelings to be dependent completely on what we think and on what we have stored within all the neuro-networking within our bodies. (More on this in Chapter 5).[56]

If we rest in the truths discussed above, those thoughts *will* affect our feelings. In fact, if we let the biblical truths about our identity in Yeshua permeate our minds, we will want to shout them from the mountaintops! However, throughout this journey of growth, there will be times when we do not feel the reality of our new identity. In those times, we need to rely on biblical truth. In doing so, do not be surprised when feelings of great joy and peace come. Our point is not to wait for our feelings and emotions to appreciate these amazing truths. We are to accept them by faith because they come from the very mouth of God and are not dependent on how we experience them.

As we conclude this section, we would like to furnish one more quote, an appropriate statement from Neil Anderson, a

---

[55] Lloyd-Jones, *Romans*, 40.

[56] If anyone would like to explore this design, we have created a place to study how it is that we will live within the experience of truth. We are speaking of the MBT Academy. MBT stands for Modular Biblical Training). The MBT Academy is an online Academy designed to help us to grow the mind that matches our reality in Messiah. You can find out about this at the end of this book.

popular author who understands what it means to be a new creation in Messiah. Anderson writes:

> The moment you believed in the Messiah, the old sinful self you inherited from Adam was gone...it's not what you do as a believer that determines who you are; it is who you are that determines what you do.[57]

---

[57] Neil T. Anderson, *Stomping Out the Darkness*, 39.

CHAPTER 5

GOD'S WORD AND NEUROSCIENCE

We noted earlier in this book that when Paul speaks of our new identity in Yeshua, he uses a few phrases that we think need more explanation. One of these phrases was "the old man." This has already been explored at length. Let us proceed to discussing the other difficult expressions.

The Body of Sin

New research in the field of neuroscience has provided valuable insight into how our mind and body are related. From the perspective of our new identities in Yeshua, this insight can help explain more fully how our minds and bodies also transition from the "old man" that died on the cross, to the new neurological wiring and anatomical make-up of our new creation in Yeshua. To do so, we need to explore some key spiritual and anatomical concepts that Paul utilizes in Romans.

First, is "the body of sin," found in Romans 6:6 where Paul says, "the old self [man] was crucified with [Yeshua], in order that our body of sin might be done away with, so that we would no longer be slaves to sin."

The expression "body of sin" should not be regarded as equivalent to a "sinful body," for the body itself is not sinful. The concept of a "sinful body" comes from the Gnostic idea that the human body and anything associated with it in this world is sinful. This has nothing to do with Paul's expression "body of sin." Paul's phrase "body of sin" derives from two very pertinent Greek words. The first is soma, soma. Soma simply means "body." It is speaking of human anatomy. The second is *harmartia*, αμαρτια. This word means "missing the mark." It is the most common Greek word translated as "sin." *Harmartia* corresponds to the most common Hebrew word for sin, *chata*, (חטא) which means "to miss the mark".

Our Flesh

The Apostolic Scriptures frequently use the Greek term *sarx*, (σαρξ), meaning "flesh," as conceptually associated with "sin" (*harmartia*). *Sarx* has a variety of uses, however, all of them can be broken down to some sort of physical or anatomical association. Moreover, just like the expression "body of sin" is used by Paul, so also do we find the words "the body of the flesh," *tou somatos teis sarkos*, του σωματος της σαρκος found in Colossians 2:11. As we can see, the Apostolic writers found association between sin and something within our anatomy, like flesh. According to Hegg, the phrase used in Colossians 2:11 "combines the sense of mortality and depravity so that the 'body of flesh' is put off through union with the Messiah in faith even as the flesh is 'put off' in the ritual of circumcision."[58] Hegg is suggesting that just as actual physical flesh is removed during circumcision,

---

[58] Tim Hegg, *Paul's Epistle to the Romans*, Vol. 2, 145. In trying to understand what is meant by *sarx* in the letters we suggest that we not use the term "sinful nature." The term "sinful nature" is often used to try to communicate the meaning of sarx. We suggest that it is not the best term to use. The term itself is not a biblical expression. It does not appear in the Greek. Some translations use this term to rendering sarx in this way. For example, see Romans 7:5, 18, and 25, among other places in the NIV. We think it is more helpful to examine what the Scriptures are saying in each context when referring to our flesh (sarx), rather than using the expression "sinful nature." This phrase tends to cause believers to think that there is still a sinful nature within them. We are suggesting that we can understand the dynamics of sarx within us without thinking that we have a "sinful nature" as part of who we are as new creations. Remember that the old person who was constituted a sinner has died with Messiah!

so too is the flesh of the "old man" removed when our identity is united with Yeshua. The body of flesh is "put off" — it exists but it no longer touches the new creation in Messiah. Why? Because according to Colossians 2:11, the flesh was circumcised from him.

Once born again, we exist inside Messiah and "the body of flesh cannot touch us." If, at times, we walk in the flesh," it is not the new creation that we are. When we "walk in the flesh", we are responsible for those actions because we did not "take every thought captive" as 2 Corinthians 10:5 explains. In other words, we demolish arguments and every pretension that sets itself up against the knowledge of God, and we take captive every thought to make it literally "under hearing" to Messiah.

As new creations we don't just shed off old flesh, we also start exercising our mind in new ways to be like the mind of Messiah (1 Corinthians 2:16). In our new life, we must physically grow a new mind that matches our new identity in Messiah.

In addition, the Apostolic writers seem to use *sarx* in two ways; some passages refer to human anatomy as "our flesh," while others refer to human behavior, still calling it "our flesh." Why does God use the same word *sarx*, which denotes an physical element, when speaking about behavior? Why does He refer to our behavior as anatomy? To explore these questions, we need to walk down a surprising trail, and pull from advances in neuroscience.

Because of the finished work of Messiah, we are new creations (2 Corinthians 5:17) and the flesh of the "old man" has been put off, or circumcised, from our bodies. But the mind of the "old man" remains. We'll call this the "old mind." This mind is still stored in the neural networks that make up the physical brain. New research in several fields of science now show how the mind is connected to the body through neural connections. The neurons of our brain are interconnected with the heart and the organs of our gut. Indeed, God created everything to be connected in the anatomy of our body.

The Amazing Brain[59]

According to Dr. John Kelly, "the brain has over eighty-six billion nerve cells or neurons with trillions of interconnections. Information is transmitted along these brain cells in tiny electrical signals. Each cell then transmits the information to connecting cells."[60] It is among these neurons that thinking takes place, including decision-making, among a host of other things. Thinking and decision-making is a physical (conscious) action taking place within a neural brain. We can make correct or detrimental decisions; contemplate godly or ungodly thoughts.

So, how does all of this relate to Paul's concept called "the body of sin" or the soma of *sarx* (the body of flesh)? If neural networks are connecting the mind and the physical body, then the "old mind" of the "old man" is still stored within the anatomy of the brain even after someone becomes a believer and enters into his new identity. It is this remaining "old mind" within a new creation that is meant by the soma of *sarx* (body of flesh).

The meaning of soma of *sarx*, however, goes even deeper. It also refers to the neural networks within the brain activity of the "old man" that still exist in the new creation believer. Therefore, "walking in the flesh," literally means giving room and liberty to the detrimental and ungodly thoughts of the "old mind" that are still functioning in our brains and active in our neural network. And because the mind and body are

---

[59] We are not neuroscientists! We owe a great deal to the following who helped us to understand the human brain, at least two of which are believers: Dr. John Kelly, a physician who became an education specialist and Dr. Caroline Leaf. Other helpful names include Dr. Andrew Huberman, a neuroscientist, and Dr. Jordan Peterson, a clinical psychologist. Please note that though we do not share all of their viewpoints, nevertheless, they are extremely helpful in their fields.

[60] John Kelly, *Whole Brain Learning and Teaching*, 18. Dr. Kelly's organization is called *Fingerprint Learning*. It uses the most advanced findings of neuroscience to help students of all ages find their own particular learning styles and find success in learning through that. www.fingerprintlearning.com

connected, the "old mind" remains a central component to our anatomy — even while we are shedding off the old flesh.

The "old mind" connected to our "flesh" is contrary to The Spirit of God (*Ruach haKodesh*, רוח הקודש). Therefore, walking according to the thought of the "old mind" is referred to in Scriptures as "walking in the flesh" and not in the Spirit. Hegg writes in this regard, "Paul uses the phrase 'according to the flesh' (*kata sarka*, κατα σαρκα 21 times in the Pauline literature) to mean life lived apart from the power of the Spirit, or life within the realm of sinful depravity."[61]

We know that the "old man" of sin was connected to the "old mind." When that person was crucified in Messiah, and received new birth, that old man literally left the body. However, the *mind* of that person remains as anatomy within the brain. That is why we sometimes experience life as *if* we are still the "old man" even though God's Word is completely clear that the old person is no longer there. Remember, "The old has gone, the new has come" (2 Corinthians. 5:17). Therefore, we can only live true to our new life by forming a new mind — a mind that matches our new identity.

The thoughts and emotions stored in the "old mind" are stored on the cellular level. The body itself, therefore, is not sinful, only what is stored within the cellular capacities of our body from our former lives. That is the only place where sin dwells in us. That is the *sarx*. When the Bible speaks of our *flesh* as sinful, it is referring to this. After all, Paul said in Romans 7:17–18a, "So now, no longer am I the one doing it, but sin which dwells in me. For I know that nothing good dwells in me, that is, in my flesh...."

As we have already indicated, in Hebrew the most common biblical word that we translate "sin" is *chatah*, (חטא). *Chatah* simply means "missing it," derived from a verb that means "missing the mark." Though Paul might have been thinking in Hebrew, he was writing in Greek. Sure enough, the

---

[61] Hegg, *Romans, Vol I*, 145.

Greek word translated sin (*hamartia*, αμαρτια) also means to "miss the mark."[62] One who practices *hamartia*, or *chatah*, or sin, is therefore "missing it!"

We need to ask, what is it that we are missing when we sin? Simply stated, we are missing our new life! We are missing our authentic self. We are missing what it is to experience the new reality of the finished work of Messiah. We are also missing others around us. We are even missing who God truly is. Walking in the flesh means we are missing out on who we were created to be, all that we were created to live, all that we are created to experience. Essentially, our Creator is trying to give us back our own life!

The Thought Trees

Let us return to our discussion about the brain. The mind of a person is made of all the neural networks that were developed since the formation of the brain within the womb. Neuro-scientists have the technology to see the neurons of our mind. The tree-like structure of neurons, seen in Figure 1, tell us why they have the nickname, "our thought trees."[63]

Figure 1: A Neuron

---

[62] Joseph Henry Thayer, *Thayer's Greek-English Lexicon of the New Testament*, entry #266: αμαρτια.
[63] The artwork in the Figures 1–5 is by Esther (Seungwon) Kim of South Korea. seungwon86@gmail.com

Furthermore, each neuron is designed to connect with others, as we see in Figures 2-3. When this happens, they are called *neuro-networks* or *neural pathways*.

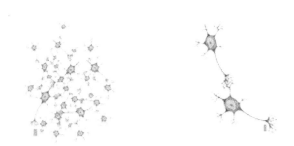

Figures 2-3: Neuro-Networks

Now, let's talk about the "branches" of a thought tree. The neurons are made of protein. Each neuron has many branches like a tree, as seen in Figure 4. These are called dendrites. Every new thought forms a new dendrite, or branch, on the neurons. With every thought, therefore, the anatomy of the brain changes. This is a reflection of the phenomenon called *neuro-plasticity.*

Figure 4: A Neuron "Thought Tree" with Dendrites

To walk in newness of life, we must form a new mind that matches our new identity. 1 Corinthians 2:16 tells us that we, as new creations, have the mind of Messiah. Therefore, to create a mind in Messiah we must think within the truths of our new identity. These truths become new thoughts, which become new dendrites on the neuron, which then links to other neurons in the neuro-networks establishing new thought patterns of the brain, which, in effect, literally becomes the new *anatomy* of our brain. The new mind forming within our brain is now an imprint of the "Mind of Messiah" within our new identities.

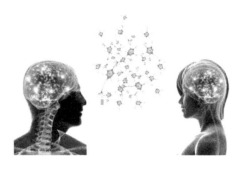

Figure 5

Figure 5 attempts to illustrate how the new mind is formed. The illustration shows the neuro-networks of a male and female in action, where every light is a thought. The image of the neuro-network between the faces represents the thought patterns of our new shared identities in the heavenlies. Each individual will have their own profound insights. The reality, however, is that we all have the same truths about our new minds and identities as described in His Word.

The Mind of Messiah

How do we get a mind that will match our new reality in Messiah? First, we need to know that 1 Corinthians 2:16 tells us that we, as new creations, have the mind of Messiah. Because that is our new reality in Messiah, we can do as our Creator instructs when He says to "set your mind on things above" (Colossians 3:2–3). As we are doing that, proteins are forming branches of trees that are filled with that which we are created to eat of! This then is the mind of Messiah forming as the anatomy of our brain. That makes a mind that matches our reality in that which is above! Along these lines, notice what we are told in Philippians 4:8,

> Finally, brothers, whatsoever things are true, whatsoever
> things are honest, whatsoever things are just, whatsoever
> things are pure, whatsoever things are lovely, whatsoever

things are of good report; if there be any virtue, and if there be any praise, think on these things.

The text says, "Think on these things!" What is happening while we are thinking on these things? Again, proteins are forming branches of trees that become the anatomy of our brain making a mind that matches our reality in that which is above! We know we have repeated ourselves. However, sometimes that is essential to help these important concepts to find their home in our thinking!

Now we are free to choose from which mind we will live! 2 Corinthians 10:5 says to take every thought captive to be "under the hearing of the Messiah." Most translations will say "to be under the obedience of Messiah." The Greek term translated "obedience" is the word *hupakoe* (υποκοη). It literally means to be "under hearing."

What is this saying to us? Let us make this personal: I choose to be "under hearing," meaning, to be in the place of hearing my new mind. As I walk a day of my life, I choose my thoughts. I need to choose my thoughts to match my new reality in Messiah. How does that happen? Romans 12:2 tells us the answer. It says simply, "Be transformed by the renewing of your mind." Our minds become renewed when we fill them with God's Word, the Scriptures.

Let us put this into both biblical and neurological terms. According to our Creator's design, if we grow neural networks that match our new reality in Messiah as God's Word describes it, we will experience ourselves in that reality. We will find ourselves free to live our life from that reality. This is what is meant when it is said that we walk in newness of life.

As we have mentioned earlier, amazingly, neuroscientists also tell us that the neuro-networks of our brain are connected to our heart and to the organs of our gut — even on a cellular level. Thus, both our heart and inner organs also have neurons. All of this neural network connectiveness is *sarx*, anatomy.

Let us word it personally again: The person who lived in my body before I was born from above, that person had a mind that was anatomy within my brain and interconnected anatomically throughout my body. The person that I once was, the old me, was by nature and birth independent and rebellious toward God. The mind of that person was then also independent and rebellious toward God. The old me is now gone, but the mind that is independent and rebellious toward God is still anatomy within my brain.

Did we get that? The person that we once were is gone. But the mind of that person is still anatomy in our brains and connected throughout our bodies. Sin dwells in the mind of the person we once were. Since this mind is anatomy in our bodies, this mind is what the Bible calls, "the body of sin," *the soma of sarx.*

Once we are born from Above, we are to begin to grow a new mind that matches our new reality in Messiah. We will have the mind of who we once were and the new mind that is growing to match our new reality as one born from Above. The Scriptures tell us that once we are born again, we have the mind of Messiah. Within the new creation us, we have the mind of Messiah. Now that mind must become the mind in our brain and begin to connect throughout all our body. Once that happens, then in daily life, we choose to use that mind and not the mind of who we once were. To understand further let us take a look at two passages of Scripture.

Colossians 3:1–4:

The first pertinent passage is Colossians 3:1–4. It reads:

> Since, then, you have been raised with Messiah, set your hearts on things above, where Messiah is seated at the right hand of God. Set your minds on things above, not on earthly things. For you died, and your life is now hidden

with Messiah in God. When Messiah, who is your life, appears, then you also will appear with Him in glory.[64]

This passage begins with a Greek conditional clause: If we have been raised with Messiah (which we have), then the implication is that we will continue seeking things above (which we do). Verse 3:2 caries the same thrust. Since we have been raised with Messiah, then we are to continually think about the things above. The word we are translating as "think about" is from the Greek verb, *phroneo* (φρονεω). It stresses the idea of giving careful consideration to something, or to set one's mind on and be intent on something.[65] Moreover, this verb is also a present imperative, meaning that we are instructed to continually set our minds on things above. This we can do because, as 3:3 states "we have died" to the "old man."

Here, like Romans 6, Paul is using the aorist tense again, indicating that our death is history. It is a once-for-all event that has already happened. And our resultant new life is now hidden in Messiah (we have the mind of Messiah neurologically connected throughout our bodies). Hence, Colossians is further teaching us to continually grow a mind that matches our new identity in Him. That is not only what we must do, but it is also what we can do because we are new people in Messiah and are forever united with Him.

Romans 6:6-7 and 12

The second relevant passage is Romans 6:6-7 and 12.

> ...knowing this, that our old self was crucified with Him, in order that our body of sin might be done away with, so that we would no longer be slaves to sin; for the one who

---

[64] Colossians 3:3 should read, "For you died and your life is hidden with Messiah in God." Some translations, however, insert the word "now" before the word "hidden." This is to help the reader distinguish between the tenses of the two verbs in this verse. The first verb "died" in Greek is in the aorist tense, a past tense, and the second verb, "hidden" is in the present tense in Greek: "For you died, and your life is now hidden with Messiah in God."

[65] BDAG, 1065.

has died is freed from sin. ... Therefore, sin is not to reign
in your mortal body so that you obey its lusts...

Here we are told that the death of the "old man" made it
possible for the body of sin to be done away with. Moreover,
the Greek verb *katargeo*, καταργεω, in English as "might be
done away with," is more accurately translated as "being
rendered powerless," or even "rendered useless."[66]

In addition, the verb *katargeo* in Romans 6:6 is in the
subjunctive mood. That is the mood of possibility. In other
words, the text teaches us that it is possible for the body of
sin to be rendered powerless. Why is it possible? For two
reasons. First, its source of power is dead. The sinner we once
were has died with Yeshua. Second, Yeshua now lives in us,
and we have His mind. We are no longer slaves to sin; we can
live His life in us and through us. That reality is reflected in
Romans 6:12, where Paul instructs us: "Therefore do not let
sin reign in your mortal body so that you obey its lusts..."
Knowing our new identities in Messiah helps us to live in the
new reality of being free from the domination of sin.

Summary

We know this chapter was rather technical. However, it
was necessary that we have a clear understanding of the
biblical concepts of the "old man," "the body of sin," "mind of
Messiah," and "sin." We suggest that the reader peruse this
chapter several times to have a better grasp of how we see
these concepts, especially how modern neuroscience sheds
amazing light of these biblical constructs. Of course, Paul did
not have the benefit of understanding these things
scientifically. Yet, he took God at His Word, applied what he
heard from the Lord, lived an amazing life — and taught
others to do the same. It is possible!

Hence, we are now in a better position to go on to Chapter
6: "Our New Identity."

---

[66] BDAG, 525.

CHAPTER 6
OUR NEW IDENTITY

So far, we have explored who we were before we trusted in Yeshua. Next, we saw what God did to change that situation, how He brought us to Himself. Then, we focused on what Yeshua did for us by uniting us with Him in His death, burial, and resurrection. All of this leads us back to the beginning of our quest. We ask once again, "Who are we?" We have concluded that it is not accurate to identify ourselves as "sinners." If that is true, then what *can* we say about ourselves now that we trust in Yeshua? This chapter aims to look at some of the clearest passages in the Bible that declare our present identity. We will explore these passages in the order in which they appear in the Scriptures.

We are Holy.

The word "holy" means the same as "sanctified." In the Torah, both words reflect the Hebrew word group associated with *kodesh*, (קודש). *Kodesh*, as well as its other grammatical variants, means to be set apart. It does not necessarily indicate any intrinsic moral or ethical quality; the emphasis is on the idea of being separate for God's use.

We see this in the extra-biblical uses of the same word, especially from Ugarit, a coastal Canaanite city. Their language was similar to Hebrew. Years ago, the ancient city of Ugarit was discovered and with it a horde of inscriptions written in

Ugaritic, a cognate language to Biblical Hebrew. They used the word "holy" to designate Canaanite temple prostitutes that were set apart for use in the temples. To be sure, they were not moral, but certainly set apart.

In the Torah, people, objects, places, and designated times are all emphasized as holy. For example, some days and years are called holy (Leviticus 23:2 and 25:12). The Tabernacle (and later the Temple) was a holy place, and certain sections of the Tabernacle were reserved for certain people, and during certain times. That would have meant that these things are all holy. Since the Tabernacle and then Temple was God's House, those structures were set apart for special uses. Moreover, the priests who participated in these holy structures wore special clothing that was referred to as holy (Exodus 28:2 and 29:29).

An exciting element about God is that He not only sees His chosen people as holy, but He *declares* them holy — it is part of their essential identity. Exodus 19:6 speaks of Israel as a holy nation. Exodus 22:31 talks about holy men to the Lord. Leviticus 11:44–45, 19:2, 20:7, 20:26, 21:6–7, and more, refer to the fact that individual people can be holy — because their God is holy.

Believers in Yeshua are called "saints" over forty times in the Apostolic Scriptures. Being called a saint means the same as being called holy. In short, God's people are those who are set apart for the Holy God. We do not just have holy attributes; we are holy at the core. That is our identity. If we are believers in Yeshua, we are saints (holy ones) and not sinners.

We Have Torah Written on Our Minds.   Jeremiah 31:31

Jeremiah was a prophet to Israel and Judah approximately 600 years before Yeshua. He had a dreadful message for Judah, castigating them for their unfaithfulness to covenant and warning them of impending disaster as a result. To be sure, Jeremiah was an eyewitness to Judah's spiritual downfall and the consequent onslaught by the Babylonians who destroyed Jerusalem, including the 1st Temple, and carried thousands away in exile to Babylon.

Suppose we were living in Israel during those tumultuous times. Suppose that we were among the countless righteous ones, that believing remnant who did not forsake their relationship with God and His Covenant. It must have been very discouraging for them to live among such a wayward people and to see the demise of their nation. Moreover, the unfaithfulness of the people and the Babylonian onslaught would have made it easy for them to think that the Holy One broke Covenant with their nation, severing their relationship and annulling the Sacred Covenant Promises.

It this context, Jeremiah preached some of the most hopeful words to the people of Judah (Jeremiah 31:31–37.) He assured them, especially the faithful remnant, that not only is the covenant relationship with the Lord intact, but God even promises to renew the covenant.

We use the term "renew" in referring to the covenant about which Jeremiah speaks, rather the more common term "new." This is a purposeful selection of wording. We are saying that neither the Book of Hebrews nor any other part of the Apostolic Scriptures represents a covenant that annuls or abrogates the covenants that God previously made with His people in the Torah. Instead, the best way to view the contents of the Newer/Renewed Covenant is to see this covenant as a renewal of the covenants already ratified.

In Jeremiah 31:31, the prophet refereed to this newer covenant by the Hebrew words, *brit chadasha* (ברית חדשה). A good linguistic case can be made for the Hebrew word "new," *chadash* (חדש), to be rendered "renew." In Hebrew, the words for "month" and "new" have the same spelling, only the vowels are slightly different. They are sister words. In the Hebrew and biblical mind, a new month is determined by the *renewing* appearance of the moon in the sky after its short period of apparent absence. What happens every month? Do we get a brand-new moon? No, of course not. Each month, through a cycle of waxing and waning, the appearance of the moon is merely *renewed*. Hence, what Jeremiah seems to be saying is that God will renew His existing covenant relationship with His people, not annul it or establish a different one.

With whom will the covenant be renewed? Jeremiah tells us in 31:32, that the renewed covenant will "not be like the covenant which I made with their fathers in the day I took them by the hand to bring them out of the land of Egypt, My covenant which they broke." That covenant, which was made at Mt. Sinai, and included people who were both followers of the true God, and those who went astray during the journey. That is why Jeremiah stated in the same verse that they "broke that Covenant."

Jeremiah 31:33–34 makes it clear that God will renew this covenant only with those who truly follow Him and believe in Yeshua as the Messiah. He says in 31:34, "They will not teach again, each man his neighbor and each man his brother, saying, 'Know the Lord,' for they will all know Me, from the least of them to the greatest of them, declares the Lord." To put it in more familiar terms, the Lord would renew the covenant with a people who would have no need for evangelism. They will all know Him in the deepest personal sense.

To underscore this important point, look at the terms of The Renewed Covenant in Jeremiah 31:33–34. The Holy One says of those who are participants:

- They will have the Lord as their God.
- They shall be His people.
- God will forgive their sin.

Each of these covenant terms have already been promised to Israel, and the believing remnant experienced them as their reality. For example:

1. *"I will be their God and they shall be my people."*

This promise is not a new promise. We read in Exodus 6:7

what God promised to the Israelite slaves in Egypt long ago when He said, "I will take you for My people and I will be your God."

2. *"I will forgive their iniquity and remember their sin no more."*

This is also not a new promise. As one might expect, we also find it in the pages of the Torah, although in a slightly different form. When Moshe went to the Lord to receive another copy of the Mt. Sinai Covenant following the golden calf incident, the Holy One, in one of the most powerful biblical statements concerning His nature to forgive sin said: "The Lord, the Lord God, is compassionate and gracious, slow to anger, and abounding in loving-kindness and truth, who keeps loving-kindness for thousands, who forgives iniquity, transgression, and sin." (Exodus 34:6.) Indeed, when Jeremiah promised that in the Renewed Covenant God would forgive sin, the Israelites already had a deep sense of this because of the explicit instructions from Moshe.[67]

3. *"I will put My Torah within them and on their heart, I will write it."*

We need to note a few important details about this promise. First, most English translations state "I will put my Law within them..." But the Hebrew term frequently translated as "law" is *Torah* (תורה). It is a mistranslation because Torah is simply a common Hebrew word that means "teaching" or "instruction," not "law." This is why Torah is also the name given to the Five Books of Moshe (Genesis, Exodus, Number, Leviticus, Deuteronomy). Look, for example, at the Hebrew wording in Deuteronomy 28:61, 29:21, and 30:10 where Moshe is writing *Sefer haTorah,* (ספר התורה), the "Book of the Torah."

Second, Jeremiah says that the Holy One will write this Torah in their innermost being — deep inside of them. This

---

[67] This quote and the other information about the covenant renewal are taken from the authors' book *Torah Rediscovered.*

is the best way of understanding the Hebrew phrase, *b'kirbam* (בקרבם). Then, He will also write the Torah "on their hearts." However, rather than translating the Hebrew word *lev* (לב) as "heart," which is usually done, we should render it as "mind." According to Dr. Eldon Clem, head of the Semitic Language Department at Jerusalem University College in Jerusalem, Israel, in the Tanakh, when the Hebrew word *lev* is used in the context of the physical organ that pumps blood, it is to be translated as heart. But when the context is not about the heart organ, *lev* means "mind."[68] This implies that we are people characterized by having God's Word inscribed in our innermost being and on our minds. Moreover, this is also not a new promise; Moshe spoke about it in Deuteronomy 30:14.

The point is, we are not the same people we once were. Before Yeshua, we were sinners from our innermost being. Now, because of what Yeshua did for us, we are people who have the Torah written in our innermost being and on our minds. It is not that we strive to obey it, as if it were a list of tasks that we check off when they are finished. Instead, since it is written in our innermost being, living it comes naturally from within. Torah, as well as the rest of the Word of God, is part of our essential new creation identity.

We Have Been Justified and Declared Righteous.   Romans 5:12–21

Leaving Jeremiah, and jumping ahead about 600 years, Paul has more to say about our present identity in Messiah. As already noted, the word "justification" or "justified" appears many times in his letter to the Romans. It is one of the many core words in the book, if not the most dominate. Romans 5:12–21 contains a summary of Paul's teaching on justification. In these verses, he makes several important points relative to our subject of identity.

Paul says in Romans 5:19, "For as through the one man's disobedience the many were made sinners." Our first parents,

---

[68] Based on personal conversations with Dr. Clem on numerous occasions throughout 2007.

Adam and Eve, sinned; they transgressed God's Words. They became sinners and everyone born since Adam and Eve were born sinners. To use Paul's terminology, they became unrighteous.[69]

Paul spoke in terms of identity when he stated that all who are in Adam "were made sinners." Paul used the Greek word *katestathasan* (κατεσταθησαν), which means to cause someone to experience something or to make someone into something.[70] Grammatically it is an aorist passive indicative verb. This means that they were caused to become sinners from a one-time action.

However, Paul continued to stress that, just as all who are in Adam became sinners or unrighteous, in like manner do all who are in Messiah become righteous or justified by God. Hence, Paul says in Romans 5:19, "even so through the obedience of the One the many will be made righteous." In this verse, "the One" is a reference to Yeshua. Paul is speaking of our essential make-up, and identity. For those still in Adam, their identity remains that of a sinner. But all who are in Yeshua — who place their trust in what He did — will be justified and made righteous in their identity.

How can God declare us to be righteous? Boice answers, "Only on the grounds of Jesus' own perfect righteousness imputed to us. That is, we are justified by God by grace alone."[71] He continues to assert that:

> Justification is an act of God as judge by which He declares us to be in a right standing before Him so far as His justice is concerned. So, the only way by which we can be declared to be in a right standing before God is on the basis of the death of [Yeshua the Messiah] for our sins, He bearing our

---

[69] It is helpful to note that in both Hebrew and Greek, the words justified and righteous are related to each other.
[70] BDAG, 492.
[71] Boice, *Romans* 604.

punishment, and by the application of [Messiah's] righteousness to us by God's grace.[72]

This raises an interesting problem. If Boice is correct when he says that "We are not just in ourselves, of course,"[73] then, on what basis can a sinner be declared to be righteous, and God still be just, honest, and fair? Theologian John Murray presents an interesting answer:

> The mere notion of declaring to be righteous is seen to be inadequate of itself to express the fullness of what is involved in God's justification of the ungodly. In God's justification of sinners there is no deviation from the rule that what is declared to be is presupposed to be. He constitutes the ungodly righteous, and consequently can declare them to be righteous.[74]

What an enormous statement. Murray is saying that before God declares people to be righteous in Yeshua, He must actually change them from within. Sinners were changed from being sinners to being righteous. Then — and only then — could God justly declare them to be acquitted of their sins. Hence, we not only have righteousness or justification, but we are also actually made by God to be righteous or justified.

We are not Condemned.   Romans 8:1

On the basis of being constituted righteous, the judge of all mankind can state from His holy and eternal bench of justice, "Therefore there is now no condemnation for those who are in Yeshua the Messiah" (Romans 8:1). Thus, we are constituted righteous and not condemned. We are acquitted from our sins.

Boice, in addition to helping us to understand righteousness, also helps to clear up some misconceptions about being condemned by God. He writes,

> Does the act of condemnation make them [people]

---

[72] Boice, *Romans,* 603.
[73] *Ibid.*
[74] John Murray, *Redemption Accomplished and Applied,* 122–123.

lawbreakers? To use biblical terminology: Does it make them sinners? Or does it merely mean that they are declared to be such? The answer is: It means that they are *declared* to be sinners. They are lawbreakers already. The act of condemnation merely declares this to be so and subjects them to whatever penalty the law in the case prescribes.[75]

It is also true of being righteous. We are already changed to be righteous. That is why God can now *declare* us to be so.

We are Accepted.   Romans 15:7

God's acceptance of us is another important aspect of our new identity.

It is true that God cannot accept sin in His presence. That is why He must condemn the unrighteous. However, Romans 15:7 reminds us of the difference in Yeshua. Paul says, "Therefore, accept one another, just as Messiah also accepted us to the glory of God." Here Paul exhorts believers to accept one another. The Greek word that Paul uses (*proslambanesthe*, προσλαμβανεσθε) is an imperative (a command) that means "to extend a welcome, receive in(to) one's home or circle of acquaintances."[76] It is a beautiful concept — to be accepting of each other in the body of Messiah.

The exciting aspect of this is that our acceptance of people in the Body of Messiah is that God also accepts us. That means that we are no longer those who are characterized by sin, but we are those whose essential constitution has been changed. Thus, we stand with the Holy One complete and accepted by Him.

We are Seated with Messiah.   Ephesians 2:5–6

Every believer in Yeshua dreams of "going to heaven"

---

[75] Boice, *Romans*, 604.
[76] BDAG, 883.

when they die.[77] However, do we have to wait that long? Fascinatingly, Paul tells the Ephesians "…even when we were dead in our transgressions, [God] made us alive together with Messiah … and raised us up with Him, and seated us with Him in the heavenly places in Yeshua the Messiah." Yes, we read it correctly, we are now, presently, "seated with Him in the heavenly places." Confessedly, that is not an easy concept to unpack.

Notice the familiar sequence of events. First, our Father made us alive with Messiah (Ephesians 2:5). Second, we are risen with Messiah (2:6). We have discussed both of these blessings before. However, third, Paul sates that God now "seated us with Messiah" (2:6).

The verb translated "seated" is in our familiar aorist tense, and it is passive. That means that we have already been made to sit with God in Messiah. That is our position now. We do not have to wait for the future, after we die, to be "in heaven." That is where we have arrived now. We live in Him here on earth and at the same time we live in Him there, in the invisible realm. When we walk in our new creation, it is a reflection of our life seated next to God in the invisible realm. Furthermore, we are seated on a throne, which means that we reign with Him. We are inside the realm of His reign where we can be confident and secure in the sovereign reign of God.

All of this, of course, speaks of victory. It involves security, privilege, and rejoicing. That is not only what we *have* in Messiah; it is *who we are.*

We are Complete.   Colossians 2:10

Colossians 2:10 states, "…and in Him you have been made complete." The word that we translate as "have been made complete" is one word in Greek: *pepleromenoi*, πεπληρωμενοι.

---

[77] We are using a familiar Christian expression, "going to heaven," for the sake of our argument here. Biblically speaking we do not await life 'in heaven", rather we await life in the world to come or "eternal life." However, it is beyond the scope of this book to explain all of this.

The root of this word can also be rendered as "full" as well as "complete." It can carry the idea of bringing to "completion that which was already begun."[78]

Earlier in the text, Paul said that Yeshua "established us in our faith" (Colossians 2:7). When God brought us to Himself and granted us the gift of salvation, He also established us and grounded us in Messiah. By this, Paul says that we are complete in Him. We lack nothing. Moreover, in Colossians 2:10, Paul uses a participle to express how we are complete in Messiah, in that we do not need to seek any further spiritual or mystical experience. We rest in the work He has done for us and is doing in us right now. One commentator states it like this:

> God intends to flood the lives of men and women, and ultimately the whole creation, with his own love, power and richness, and that He has already begun to put this plan into effect through Messiah and by His Spirit. That is the Colossians' inheritance in Messiah, and they can want nothing more from any other source.[79]

> Lloyd-Jones also comments on this aspect of our lives when he says: "We," says Paul, "were baptized into Messiah Yeshua"; and he says elsewhere, "We are complete in Him" (Colossians 2:10).

> When? Now! Not, we *shall* be complete in Him, but we are complete in Him now.[80]

King David even wrote about this completeness in Psalm 23:1–3. We will include here a more literal translation:

> The Lord is My Shepherd, I experience nothing as missing ... He leads me upon waters of rest, He returns my whole self, back to me (our translation).

We are Forgiven, Redeemed, Saved, Reconciled, and More.

When we hear of such words as we have expressed in this

---

[78] BDAG, 828.

[79] N. T. Wright, *Colossians* (*Tyndale Commentaries*), 109.

[80] Lloyd-Jones, *Romans 6*, 40.

section heading: forgiven, redeemed, saved, and reconciled, we know that these gifts are treasures that God gave us as gifts, out of His grace. Moreover, these are things that we *have*. Indeed, they are! We understand that this is just a partial list of the amazing grace gifts that the Holy One has bestowed on us because of Yeshua. The list can go on for a long time; we are merely mentioning the best-known of those treasures.

However, we would like to suggest something a little unordinary. Let us talk about these grace gifts a little differently. Instead of saying that "we *have* forgiveness" or "we *have* redemption," and the like, let us speak of these things in terms of defining our identity. For example, who are we? We are people who *are* redeemed. We are those who *are* forgiven; we *are* believers in Yeshua, and we *are* saved. Can we hear the difference?

We most certainly do have these treasures as part of our life in Messiah, given to us out of the grace and mercy of God to those who are most undeserving. That is absolutely true. Yet, these are such a part of us as new creations that they are part of what defines us.

CHAPTER 7

SOME IMPLICATIONS OF KNOWING
OUR NEW CREATION IDENTITY

We hope the reader has understood so far what the Scriptures teach concerning our biblical identity in Yeshua. The theme of this book, after all, is to reorient our thinking about our identities where we no longer perceive of ourselves as sinners at the core, but as saints and new creations because of what Yeshua did for us in His death, burial, and resurrection. In this chapter we will explore, in no particular order, some of the important implications of knowing our biblical identity in Yeshua.

Knowing ourselves as new creations helps us in our battle against the flesh.

In chapter 5, we went into detail discussing the "body of flesh" (*sarx*) as left-over anatomy from our former selves that still causes us to miss living out our new creation identities. We concluded that "flesh" is "the mind patterned after this world." This assertion we supported with Paul's explanation that when we sin, it is not I — the new creation — that sins but sin that dwells in my members. Here, we will look at this concept again, together with circumcision, in a new light that will help us as new creations resist sinful (fleshy) temptations.

If we carry out sin that dwells in our members, are we not still basically sinners? The answer is a resounding "No!" Why is it no? The answer is in Colossians 2:11–13. Writing to the believers in Colossae, Paul says,

> and in Him you were also circumcised with a circumcision made without hands, in the removal of the body of the flesh by the circumcision of Messiah; having been buried with Him in baptism, in which you were also raised up with Him through faith in the working of God, who raised Him from the dead. When you were dead in your transgressions and the uncircumcision of your flesh, He made you alive together with Him, having forgiven us all our transgressions… .

The key phrase in this passage is "you were circumcised." Paul is not talking about physical circumcision. He says so specifically when he spoke of circumcision as that circumcision which is "made without hands." However, to understand this unseen circumcision we need to understand physical circumcision. The physical circumcision pictures the unseen circumcision.

In physical circumcision, the flesh is removed, severed from the rest of the body. It is cut away to reveal the true organ beneath the veil of flesh. Paul says that the Holy One did the same to us in the unseen realm. When someone walks in the flesh, it is difficult for us to see the new creation that the person truly is because a veil of flesh covers them from view.

To reveal the glory of the new creation, God cuts the flesh away; it is no longer part of who we are. We have already concluded that sin is in the flesh. Hence, in Messiah, not only are we dead to sin, and not only did Messiah take it away, but the flesh is not attached to us any longer. As a result, Paul can honestly say, "it is no longer I who sins, but sin that dwells in my members." The sin that once was true of us is circumcised from us. We take responsibility for missing the mark or transgressing. But we do not take ownership for it, as if it were part of our new creation identity. Moreover, when Paul says that the flesh is circumcised, he is once again speaking in the aorist tense. It is history, never to be repeated.

The implication is that this circumcision took pace the moment we believed in Yeshua.

Thus, knowing ourselves as new creations can help us in our battle against sin. If it is no longer, we who sins, then it is easier to give it up. We do not have to linger there. We can easily forgo it and just say, no! We can say no to the temptation because it is not who we are.

Bill Gillham helps us to understand this concept when he writes:

> when Messiah died, you died. You must deal with those verses. You must deal with the question, "What died?" I have dealt with it, and arrived at the conclusion that it was the old self, the old identity that died; and have appropriated this in my own life. When I did all that, I immediately began to experience a vastly more consistent victory over life-long hang-ups.[81]

Knowing Ourselves as New Creations helps us to relate to difficult people.

In 2 Corinthians 5:16, Paul enigmatically stated, "Therefore from now on we recognize no one according to the flesh; even though we have known Messiah according to the flesh, yet now we know *Him in this way* no longer." The very next verse states: "Therefore if anyone is in Messiah, this person is a new creation; the old things passed away; behold, new things have come." In these two verses, Paul is teaching us some points about living as new creations by reminding us that new creation believers relate to each other differently than other people. Believers are called upon by the Lord not to relate to other believing brothers and sisters according to the flesh. If someone acts bitterly toward us or if someone is short tempered toward us, we are called to not respond with our flesh toward their flesh. Rather, we are to relate to their new creation self. Gillham explains this concept when he says,

---

[81] Gillham, *Lifetime Guarantee*, 73.

We must not observe a person's behavior and, from that point of reference, infer his nature. It isn't the flying that makes a bird a bird; it's his birth that makes a bird a bird. Similarly, it's not a man's adulterous behavior that identifies him as having a dead spirit...it is his birth, not his performance, that determines his identity according to the Bible.[82]

Put Offs and Put Ons

In Chapter 5 we discussed how the flesh (*sarx*), or the body of sin, is "put off," or circumcised, from our new creation bodies when we are made new creations, according to Colossians 2:11. We pick up on that concept here as Paul continued to use the phrases "put off" and "put on" when describing our new creation behavior in Ephesians 4:21–32. Here we will analyze seven of Paul's "put off" and "put on" scenarios when describing how we act toward others.

Put Off and Put On #1 – Ephesians 4:22–24

> ...in reference to your former way of life, you are to
> rid yourselves of the old self, which is being
> corrupted in accordance with the lusts of deceit, and
> that you are to be renewed in the spirit of your
> minds, and to put on the new self, which in *the
> likeness of* God has been created in righteousness and
> holiness of the truth.

Put off the old man.

The Greek grammar in these verses is very complex, containing both present and aorist infinitives and participles, which are difficult to translate. The NASB translation sounds like we must deal with the "old man," who is still alive, although that would be a direct contradiction of what Romans 6 teaches on the finished work of Messiah. The translator's note in the NET Bible is extremely helpful in that it says, "An alternative rendering for the infinitives in vv. 22–24 ('to lay aside...to be renewed...to put on') is 'that *you have* laid aside...that *you are*

---

[82] Gillham, 70.

being renewed…that *you have* put on'" (Italics ours).[83] This translation of the infinitives supports what we are saying, and what Paul said in Romans 6, that the old man has, indeed, died.

In this case, Ephesians 4:22–23 would read like this: "…that, in reference to your former manner of life, that you have laid aside the old man, which was corrupted in accordance with the lusts of deceit…that you are being renewed in the spirit of your mind…".

Based on this, we see that we do not have to put off the old man — indeed, we cannot do that; it was accomplished in the finished work of Messiah. Instead, Paul is talking about the way we think — what goes on in our minds. This is clear from verse 23 when he encouraged "to be renewed in the spirit of your minds." He wants us to mentally refuse to act as if the old man is still alive.

Put on clothes that fit.

If we have laid aside and have put off the old way of thinking, then the renewing of minds means thinking according to righteousness and truth, because we have been created in God's likeness. We are to let our minds dwell on truths concerning who we now are in Messiah, because it is these words that describe who we really are.

Put Off and Put On #2 – Ephesians 4:25

Therefore, ridding yourselves of falsehood, *speak truth each one of you with his neighbor,* because we are parts of one another.

Put off falsehood.

The language is simple. Being born from Above, we have the ability to tell the truth. We do not have to yield to falsehood any longer. In addition, if someone speaks lies to us, we are not to respond to their flesh. Rather…

Put on truthfulness.

---

[83] *The NET Bible Second Edition Notes*, comments on Ephesians 4:22.

Speak truth with your fellow companion (your "neighbor"). Zechariah 8:16 says, "These are the things which you should do: speak the truth to one another; judge with truth and judgment for peace in your gates." The prophet is describing new creation behavior.

Put Off and Put On #3 – Ephesians 4:26

> Be angry, and *yet* do not sin; do not let the
> sun go down on your anger…

Put off sin.

As above, the language here is also simple: Do not sin. In other words, put off sin. But just as we have put off the "old man" and his sinful nature when we were born again — therefore no longer identifying as a sinner — the "old mind" of the flesh (*sarx*) tends to rear its head even in our new creation bodies. We have been discussing this concept all along throughout this book. But here Paul gives us an interesting option with how to deal with the sin of the "old mind." He says, "Be angry!"

Put on anger.

Paul tells us that righteous anger is permitted, but unrighteous anger is not. The new creation is like the One who bore him. God gets angry at unrighteousness and behavior that is contrary to His character and contrary to the character of the humanity that He created!

In Ephesians 4:26, Paul bolsters his point by quoting Psalm 4:4: "Tremble, and do not sin. Meditate in your heart/mind upon your bed and be still. Selah." The word in Psalm 4:4 that we translate "tremble" could be trembling with anger, that is, being very angry even with an emotional reaction that affects our bodies. Yet, according to the Psalm writer — and Paul, who quotes this passage — it is possible to have such strong anger and yet not sin in that anger. From this we learn that while the new creation believer may certainly be angry, nevertheless, we must guard ourselves so that the flesh does not take over and rule our anger. Hence, handling our anger has a flesh way and a new creation way.

In our passage in Ephesians, Paul mentions one way that anger can be expressed through our flesh. Paul says, "do not let the sun go down on your anger" (4:26). The main reason for this is in the next phrase: "do not give the devil an opportunity" (4:27). If we let our anger continue to the next day, we provide opportunities for the evil one to tempt and lure us into transgression. For example, a seed of bitterness could grow, or we might be tempted to let a precious relationship disintegrate. That would be expressing anger in the flesh. Whereas the new creation is certainly permitted to be angry, yet the new creation handles their anger quite differently. For example, the new creation does not look at the other person after their flesh. That makes it easier to attempt to seek any necessary forgiveness and reconciliation.

Put Off and Put On #4 – Ephesians 4:28

The one who steals must no longer steal; but rather he must labor, producing with his own hands what is good, so that he will have *something* to share with the one who has need.

Put off stealing.

Everyone knows that stealing is wrong. But unfortunately, sometimes, even believers steal. That is why Paul taught about stealing to the believers in Ephesus. Stealing can take many forms. For example:

- Taking anything that does not belong to you.
- Taking credit for something you did not do.
- Taking someone else's work.
- Taking someone' else's goods.

When a believer does these things, he/she is definitely walking in the flesh. But Paul says to the new creations that they can assuredly put off these habits. At this point, notice an important detail in the text. The language says, "the one who steals." it does not call them a thief. That would be mislabeling their identity. In the flesh the person is stealing.

Rather, Paul is making an appeal to the new creation person, who although in his flesh he is capable of stealing, is not a thief.

Put on working.

The flesh steals. The new creation works. Instead of robbing others of the fruit of their labor, believers are encouraged to work for their own living. The word for "work" in Ephesians 4:28 is *kopiato* (κοπιατω) and it signifies the strenuous work that produces fatigue.[84] Thus, the new creation person works hard when it is time to work. More than that, they are to work to *be able to give to those in need.* According to Ephesians 4:28, the believers' motive for earning is not merely to have enough for oneself and one's own, but to have in order to give to the needy. That is a loving attribute of the new creation believer.

Put Off and Put On #5 – Ephesians 4:29

> Let no unwholesome word come out of your mouth,
> but if there is any good word for edification according
> to the need of the moment, say that, so that it will give
> grace to those who hear.

Put off unwholesomeness.

In verse 4:29, the word translated in the NASB as "unwholesome" (*sapros*, σαπρος) carries the idea of something being of "such poor quality as to be of little or no value, to the extent of being harmful, even bad or evil."[85] In this, Paul is teaching the new creation to be careful what comes out of our mouths. There is practically no limit to the amount of unwholesome language our mouths are able to produce when walking in the flesh — even for believers. And that is not how the new creation believers speak.

Put on edification.

Instead of yielding our mouths to the flesh in what we say,

---

[84] BDAG, 558.
[85] BDAG, 913.

the new creation speaks graciously and only that which will build others up (4:29).

This applies especially to those who are spiritual leaders, as what they say, preach, and publish, often goes public, reaching a wider audience. Therefore, their words are liable to bring the most damage to others. The new creation leader speaks words that will build others up rather than those that are judgmental or abusive, which bring people down and discourage them. We should note that Ecclesiastes 10:12 says, "Words from the mouth of a wise man are gracious, while the lips of a fool consume him."

Put Off and Put On #6 – Ephesians 4:30

Do not grieve the Holy Spirit of God, by whom you
were sealed for the day of redemption.

Put off grieving the Holy Spirit.

Well before Paul wrote to the Ephesians, the prophet Isaiah described the sorrowful condition of some of God's people in his day. Because they rebelled against the Holy One, Isaiah 63:10 records how they "grieved the Holy Spirit." They made God deeply sad by their rebellion, especially after all He graciously did for them.

The LXX translates the Hebrew verb "sad" ('*atzav*, עצב) by using the term *paroxumon*, παρωξυναν. While this is a different from Paul's "grieve," used in Ephesians 4:30, nevertheless, it carries a similar idea. Both words testify to the fact that our fleshly attitudes, speech, and behavior saddens the Holy One. In Ephesians 4:30, Paul used a present active imperative, which means it is a command. If we were not capable of doing it, the command would never be used. In addition, it is a present command, meaning we are not to "continually" grieve the Holy Spirit. When we walk in the flesh, it greatly saddens our Creator. Paul is reminding the new creation not to continually do this.

Put on our seal of ownership.

Instead of saddening our Creator, remember that He has ownership over us. Paul reminds us in Ephesians 4:30, that it is the Holy Spirit "by whom you were sealed for the day of redemption." This indicates God's ownership. We belong to God and the Holy Spirit is that token of ownership.[86] As God's personal seal of ownership, the Spirit is with us continually. Paul bids us, in a single sentence, not to grieve or sadden our Creator, but to accept His ownership over us because He has sealed us for an important event — the day of redemption.

Put Off and Put On #7 – Ephesians 4:31–32

All bitterness, wrath, anger, clamor, and slander must
be removed from you, along with all malice. Be kind to
one another, compassionate, forgiving each other, just
as God in Christ also has forgiven you.

Put off bitterness, wrath, anger, clamor, slander, malice.

Once more, the apostle turns back to those sins that so readily find expression in speech. Let us look closer at each word.

Bitterness

This refers to the resentful spirit, which refuses reconciliation.

Wrath and Anger

These two words are often used together. Earlier, we were told by Paul to put on anger (Ephesians 4:25). But in that discussion, we designated between anger from the flesh, and righteous anger from the new creation. Here, Paul is referring to anger and wrath from the flesh. This sometimes springs

---

[86] "A wax seal would have a mark of ownership or identification stamped in it, identifying who was, attesting what was inside the container that had been sealed. Because it was commonly understood that the Spirit would be made especially available in the time of the end." According to Craig Keener, Paul here speaks of the Spirit as a "deposit… a term used in ancient business documents to mean a 'down payment.' Those who had tasted the Spirit had begun to taste the life of the future world that God had promised his people." See Craig S. Keener, *IVP Bible Background Commentary*, 542.

from personal animosity, the flaring up of passion and temper because of personal provocation.

Clamor

This speaks of the loud self-assertion of the angry person, who tries to make everyone hear their grievance.

Slander

The NASB uses "slander" to translate the Greek *blasphemia* (βλασφημια). It is a word often used in the Bible for speaking against God, as one can easily see the English term "blasphemy" in this word. However, it is also common for slanderous or abusive speaking against one's fellows.

Malice

Malice is an inclusive word referring collectively to all negative, or sinful, actions already specified, and anything else of a similar kind.

Living these verses would be walking in the flesh. Paul, therefore, urges believers to put off all of these things by not walking in the flesh.

Put on...

Kindness

According to Ephesians 4:32, the new creation treats others with kindness. The lexicon defines this Greek term (*chrestoi,* χρηστοι) as being "loving and benevolent."[87] Kindness is a word that, for whatever reason, is not heard very much among believers. Kindness is both an action (how we treat others) as well as a way of speaking, i.e. speaking kindly.

Compassion

The word we translate as "tender hearted" (*eusplagchnoi,* ευσπλαγχνοι) is sometimes rendered "compassion." One prominent lexicon defines this Greek word to mean, "to have

---

[87] BDAG, 1090.

tender feelings for someone."[88] Paul's language in verse 4:32 indicates that acts of kindness will not happen without thinking sympathetically with love. It boils down to our thought life.

Forgiveness

Finally — and to wrap up the seven "put off" and "put ons" — Paul reminds the new creation to treat others with forgiveness. This is a certain remedy for any malice or bitterness in the flesh. How much forgiveness are we to have? Paul gives the answer in the last part of 4:32 when he says that we are to forgive each other "just as Messiah also has forgiven you." Since Messiah's bank account of forgiveness is unlimited, so is ours because He is the One who lives inside the new creation and enables us to grant as much forgiveness as is needed.

An Additional Thought about Forgiveness

Sometimes, unfortunately, practicing forgiveness can be a problem. In our opinion, the Scriptures teach two kinds of forgiveness. One kind we shall call *Judicial Forgiveness*. Judicial forgiveness is formally declaring to the offender that they are acquitted. This is the forgiveness we have in Messiah because of what He did for us.

However, we are not forgiven unless we believe in Yeshua. We must come to Him. When the sinner does come, as we have already indicated, God's bank account of forgiveness is unlimited! Of course, the Lord was always willing to grant forgiveness, but He could not apply that to our account until we asked for it.

The second kind of forgiveness we shall call *Practical Forgiveness*. Practical forgiveness is the kind of forgiveness we grant because of daily offenses. As far as God is concerned, 1 John 1:9 speaks of that kind of forgiveness. The Scripture says, "If we confess our sins, He is faithful and righteous to forgive

---

[88] BDAG, 413.

us our sins and to cleanse us from all unrighteousness." Let us take this apart to see what it is saying.

The first thing to note about 1 John 1:9 is the word translated "confess." In Greek the word is *homologomen*, ομολογωμεν. This term literally means "to say the same thing." In other words, when we confess our sins, we say the same thing about our sin as God is saying to us about that sin. But what does He say about our sin? The word translated sin is our familiar Greek word *hamartia*. As stated earlier, both *hamartia* and its Hebrew equivalent, *chatah*, חטאה, primarily mean "to miss the mark." The mark is God's perfect righteousness. When we walk in the flesh, we miss that mark. When we walk in the flesh, we miss our true and authentic life. Thus, to say the same thing about our sin as God does, means that we have walked in the flesh and have missed the mark.

Although this seems complex, or unorthodox, it is our Creator's way of always trying to help us know the creation that He originally intended for us.

Next, 1 John 1:9 says that when we say the same thing about our sin as God does, God is faithful and just to forgive us. Why is He faithful and just for forgive us? It is because of what Yeshua did for us on the Tree. He took our sins away. He carried them off. When He died, the sinner died and carried our sins with Him! Hence, that leaves God free to release us from the guilt of that sin — we are forgiven. That means He has granted judicial forgiveness. Yet, there is more.

The final part of the verse says that God will cleanse us from all unrighteousness. Though we have been given the gift of acquittal from the Holy Judge, nevertheless, we get soiled from our daily walk in this life. It is as Yeshua told Peter in John 13:10, "He who has bathed needs only to wash his feet, but is completely clean; and you are clean, but not all of you." Being "bathed" means that we have come to believe in Yeshua, thereby God grants judicial forgiveness. Being "not completely clean" means that we have been soiled from our daily walk.

God will cleanse us of that sin as well — all we need to do is to come to Him for it. If we are in Messiah, God says that Yeshua's death covers all of our sin. Just stop, turn, and walk back toward the Holy One!

What we have described above is what the Scriptures label by the word "repentance." We are speaking about the Hebrew word, *shuv*, שׁוּב. (Since "repentance" is a noun, the Hebrew equivalent, therefore, would be *shuvah*, שׁובה). *Shuv* as a verb can be rendered "return," "restore," and sometimes translated as "repent." It carries the idea of making a visible return to God. When we yield our members to sin, in a sense we walk away from God and His Word. The moment we realize that we are doing this, we turn and return back toward God and our true identity in Him. This process does not have to take long. It can be really quick. Figure 6 illustrates this walking away and returning.

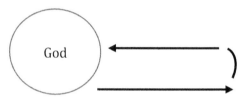

Figure 6

The same applied in our relationships with others, especially in the Body of Messiah. New creation believers should not walk by holding grudges and bitterness. If we have been offended by someone, both parties need to talk it through. If they ask for forgiveness, we should have already released them in our mind/heart, not having held a grudge against them.

On the other hand, they should not be told they are forgiven until they have asked for it. They need to acknowledge that they have offended someone. Then once they do acknowledge that they have wronged another person, outward forgiveness should be freely granted. We can say something like: "If you ask me to forgive you, there is no problem, I will!" But it is wise not to say it until they ask for it. We can do that because as new creations, we have already forgiven them in our mind/heart. In fact, we are commanded to forgive when we are asked to grant it.

EPILOGUE
THE GOOD NEWS IS BETTER THAN WE THOUGHT

When English speakers talk about the redemptive work of Yeshua, they refer to it as "The Gospel." This term is from the Greek word *euaggelion*, ευαγγελιον, which corresponds to the Hebrew word *besorah*, בשורה. Both expressions mean "good news." The verb would mean "preach the good news." This takes us back to the beginning of our book. *Besorah* is related to the word *meveseret* (מברשרת) used in Isaiah 40:9 and the verse behind the picture on the cover of this present book and discussed in the Preface.

We hope that by now the reader can understand the Good News of Yeshua in a fuller light than when this book was begun. One way to tell is to re-evaluate how the perception of our identity has changed from being sinners to a saint. For this is truly one of God's greatest miracles!

When we study how that change took place, we see how intricate the entire work of Yeshua was/is on our behalf. Central to the Good News is the reality of our eternal union with Yeshua in His death, burial, and resurrection. Studying the concept of our union with Messiah adds depth and substance to the concept that God loves us. It helps us to understand in profound ways that our Messiah loves us and how He demonstrated His love toward those who did not deserve it.

It is true that in Yeshua, our Eternal Father gave us many gifts from His grace. The list of these gifts if is just about endless. However, it is one thing to say that we have these things, like salvation, redemption, forgiveness, and other "theological" terms. It is quite another thing to say that we have become the meaning of these term by becoming a different person. We have become one who is rescued from death, one who is free from slavery to sin, and one who is a forgiven person from the very core of our being.

We have seen that if there is one biblical phrase that really sums up who we are in Messiah, it is the phrase "new creation." It implies that we have been made entirely new by the work of God. We are not people who derive our identity from listening to God. We listen to Him because of who we are. When we became believers in Yeshua, we did not simply get something, we became someone.

One final quote will be sufficient. David C. Needham understands what we have been saying and he knows how this knowledge can truly affect our daily lives. Read how he expressed his excitement at knowing the good news of the Good News: (Capital letters are all Needham's.)

> I wish I could shout these next lines around the world! A believer is not simply a person who gets forgiveness, who gets to go to heaven, who gets the Holy Spirit, who gets a new nature. Mark this—*a believer is a person who has become someone he was not before.* A believer, in terms of his deepest identity, is a SAINT, a born child of God, a divine masterpiece, a child of light, a citizen of heaven. *Not only positionally* (true in the mind of God but not true in actuality here on earth), *not only judicially* (a matter of God's moral bookkeeping) but ACTUALLY (Emphasis, Needham's).[89]

If there is ever a place for true biblical emotion, certainly this is the place to express our deepest joy at knowing that our

---

[89] David C. Needham, *Birthright*, 47. We substituted the word "believer" for his term "Christian."

eternal loving Father has sent His Son to bring us to Himself and make us into new creations who are His eternal children. Let us bask in that new identity and praise Him for that eternal gift.

MBT Academy
Modular Bibilcal Training Academy

WWW.TORAHTRUTHS.COM

The MBT Academy offers biblical training as a unique place of learning for all ages. Through the use of specially designed Power Points, we have produced a series of what we call "Sitting Rooms." These rooms utilize what we have learned from recent discoveries in neuroscience that are foundational to the process of learning. This style of learning helps to develop a biblical vocabulary and build fundamental concepts needed for learning Torah. By Torah, we mean the whole of God's Written Word — The Bible as a whole book.

The Sitting Rooms are designed for one to sit, ponder, and explore the truths presented. It is progressive; each Sitting Room prepares the student for the next Sitting Room. This is designed to first explore and then to use repeatedly, providing a lifetime of very practical help to live as we are created to live.

Today, our understanding of humanity has drifted far from

what God describes in His Word. We also have drifted far from the human relationships which God designed from the beginning. The MBTA helps to provide answers to some of our most important questions, such as:

- How can we rediscover what God created humanity to be?

- How do we know who we are as His children?

- How can we rediscover the foundations of our faith and rediscover foundations of human relationships?

- How can we rediscover our Father, our Creator?

Everything discussed in this present book is reflected in the MBTA. The student will find very practical help to grow a new mind that matches our new reality in Messiah. The MBTA provides practical help in our journey of freedom to live as we were created to live within the new creation that we are through the finished work of Messiah on the Tree. It is transformational thinking that transforms relationships. Going from one Sitting Room to the next develops depths of wisdom as together we explore "Timeless Torah Truths."

You will find The MBT Academy on this website:

torahtruths.com

Bibliography and Helpful Resources

The following is a bibliography of sources cited and other resources proven to be very helpful in writing this book. However, just because we have used a given source does not mean we necessarily agree with everything the author says or thinks. Yet, we have deemed that particular work to have a helpful contribution to the subject of the believer's identity, which is why we have included it in this bibliography.

Bible Commentaries

Boice, James Montgomery. *Romans (Boice Expositional Commentary)*. Grand Rapids: Baker Academic, 1991.

——. *God The Redeemer: Vol II of Foundations of the Christian Faith*. Madison. WI: Inter-Varsity Christian Fellowship, 1978.

Bruce, F. F. *Romans (Tyndale New Testament Commentaries)*. Nottingham: Inter-Varsity Press, 1985.

Harrison, Everett F. *Romans (Expositor's Bible Commentary)*. Grand Rapids, MI: Zondervan, 1990.

Hegg, Tim. *Paul's Epistle to the Romans: Notes and Commentary*. Vols. 1 & 2. Tacoma, WA: TorahResource, 2005.

Lloyd-Jones, D. Martyn. *Romans: Exposition of Chapter 6 — The New Man*. Edinburgh: The Banner of Truth Trust, 1992.

Murray, John. *Epistle to the Romans (New International Commentary on the New Testament)*. Grand Rapids, Eerdmans, 1980.

The NET Bible, Second Edition Notes (NET Notes). Nashville, TN: Biblical Studies Press (Thomas Nelson), 2019.

Wright, N. T. *Colossians* (*Tyndale Commentaries*). Downers Grove, Ill: Intervarsity Press, 1986.

OTHER HELPFUL BOOKS

Anderson, Neil. *Stomping Out the Darkness.* Minneapolis, MN: Bethany House, 2007.

Berkowitz, Ariel & D'vorah. *Take Hold: Embracing Our Divine Inheritance with Israel.* Richmond, MI: Shoreshim Publishing, 2020.

———. *Torah Rediscovered.* Richmond, MI: Shoreshim Publishing, 2014.

Gillham, Bill. *Lifetime Guarantee.* Brentwood, TN: Wolgemuth & Hyatt Publishers, 1987.

Kelly, John. *Whole Brain Learning and Teaching: A Practical Introduction for Learners of All Ages, Parents and Teachers.* Bangor, N. Ireland: Fingerprint Learning Ltd., 2016.

Lord, Peter. *Turkeys and Eagles.* Jacksonville, FL: The Seed Sowers, 1987.

McDowell, Josh and McDowell, Sean. *Evidence That Demands a Verdict: Life-Changing Truth for a Skeptical World.* Bletchley, Milton Keynes, UK: Authentic, 2017.

Needham, David. *Birthright.* Sisters, OR: Multnomah Publishers, 1981. (We are using the 1999 edition. The 1995 issue of this work was published under the title, *Alive for the First Time.*).

LEXICONS AND LANGUAGE STUDIES

Arndt, William F., and Gingrich, F. Wilbur. *Bauer's Greek-English Lexicon of the New Testament and Other Early Christian Literature* ("BDAG"). Chicago: The University of Chicago Press, 1957, 2000.

Brown, Francis; Driver, S. R.; and Briggs, Charles A. *The New Brown, Driver, Briggs, Gesenius Hebrew and English Lexicon* ("BDB"). Peabody, MA: Hendrickson Publishers, 1979.

Burton, Ernest D. *Syntax of The Moods and Tenses in New Testament Greek. Chicago:* The University of Chicago Press, 1893.

Dana, H. E. and Mantey, Julius R. *A Manual Grammar of the Greek New Testament.* Toronto: The Macmillan Company, 1953.

Freedman, David Noel, ed. *Eerdmans Dictionary of the Bible.* Grand Rapids: Eerdmans, 2000.

Goetchius, Eugene van Ness. *The Language of the New Testament.* New York: Charles Scribner's Sons, 1965.

Jenni, Ernst and Westermann, Claus, eds. *Theological Lexicon of the Old Testament.* Hendrickson Publishers, 1997.

Koehler, Ludwig and Baumgartner, Walter. *The Hebrew and Aramaic Lexicon of The Old Testament* ("HALOT"), Subsequently Revised by Walter Baumgartner and Johann Jakob Stamm. Translated and Edited under The Supervision of M.E.J. Richardson. Leiden, Cologne, New York: Koninklijke Brill NV, 2000.

Moulton, James Hope and Milligan, George. *The Vocabulary of the Greek Testament.* Grand Rapids: Eerdmans, 1930, 1982.

Thayer, Joseph Henry. *Thayer's Greek-English Lexicon of the New Testament.* Peabody, MA: Hendrickson, 1995.

Wallace, Daniel B. *Greek Grammar Beyond the Basics: An Exegetical Syntax of the New Testament.* Grand Rapids: Zondervan, 1996.

About the Authors

Ariel Berkowitz (B.S. West Chester State University and Philadelphia Biblical University together; M. Div. Biblical Theological Seminary; part-time courses from Rodef Torah School of Jewish Studies) and D'vorah, are instructors with Torah Resources International. Ariel has been a full-time instructor at Israel College of Bible (early 1990's). He was also an Instructor with TorahResource Institute (www.TorahResource.com). Ariel is presently an Adjunct Professor (since 1995) with The Master's University, Israeli campus ("IBEX"). Ariel and D'vorah have four grown children and seven grandchildren. They live in the northern Negev, Israel.